EMPATH AND PSYCHIC ABILITIES

A Transformative Guide with Shamanic Wisdom
and Psychological Insight to Unlock Your Secret Gifts:
Embrace Your Shadows, Awaken Your Potential,
and Become an Empowered Empath

By Sanyana Alaina

WHERE DREAMS MANIFEST
Transform your Life - Transform the World

ISBN: 978-3-9826531-1-2

FREE MEDITATION AND SPOTIFY BUNDLE

Hello beautiful Soul,

my team and I have created a special gift for you:

3 beautifully guided meditations and 7 Spotify playlists that complement the

exercises in this book and are great for practical support in working through

these exercises. I would like to offer them to you for free.

To get the download link, go to our website:

wheredreamsmanifest.com/empath

We are here to support your dream; by giving us an Amazon review,

you support ours <3 We would appreciate it very much!

To get there, just scan the QR Code below.

USA	UK	CANADA	AUSTRALIA

Thank you!

Much love to you,

Sanyana and the WHERE DREAMS MANIFEST Team

TABLE OF CONTENTS

EXERCISES IN THIS BOOK

INTRODUCTION

What if I told you that you possess actual real-life superpowers? That you can see auras, perceive thoughts, heal yourself and others with your energy, speak worlds into existence, and manifest even your wildest imagination? How would you use those abilities? And what would your life look like?

Imagine knowing precisely what is going on in a tense situation and what it takes to recreate harmony. For example, when you meet a loved one or friend and can tell with one look at their face that they are grumpy! It's bubbling underneath the surface. But when you ask them what's wrong, you only get question marks on their face. They don't know what you mean; everything is fine. As an empath—which I assume you are since you picked up this book—simply ignoring the situation won't be as easy. You likely desire to harmonize the energy when you feel tension around you, and it might seem like you are picking up on things others aren't aware of. Maybe you've been in situations where you've asked yourself: Did I just imagine that feeling?

But what if, in that situation, you could see your friend's energy? Whether they carry suppressed anger or not could be answered much easier if you could immediately check their auric field. You could quickly confirm or clarify what energy they are radiating while respecting their space if they don't want to discuss the issue. You could also check your own auric field and see if there is something that is clouding your perception. Furthermore, you could observe what circumstances, activities, or words strengthen or weaken your energy field or that of your friend, and support accordingly.

Now tell me how much easier your life could be with just the gift of auric vision. And what if I told you that this and even more magical abilities are already dormant in you, simply waiting to be unpacked?

Most likely, what you've experienced so far mainly consists of the challenges of being an empath—the high sensitivity and rapid sensory overload in noisy and busy environments. Perhaps you have often felt misunderstood or even been called crazy and oversensitive by others. In this book, I want to give you a perspective on your nature as an empath that can change your life forever because I will not only show you the fantastic potential lying dormant in you but will also assist you in unfolding it.

This way, you will get to know a whole new you throughout reading this book. A side of you that you may have never dared to dream of or wouldn't even have found realistic in your dreams if it showed up. The version of you fully in charge of your divine abilities and human emotions.

As an empath, you are gifted with the power of sensitivity and the strong desire to help and heal those around you. In this book, we will discuss what true healing means and discover ways to support your own healing journey, as well as assist others on theirs through developing and using your innate psychic gifts. With this book, I invite you to explore the secret world of magic and wonder and show you why those are not just esoteric clichés but perfectly logical and rational existential truths of life in our shared reality.

Over the last few centuries, science gradually discovered what Shamanic cultures have known for ages: the world of matter as we perceive it is only a secondary phenomenon of the underlying energy play—no witchcraft, simple physics. But our five senses are commonly trained to orient themselves on matter only and to ignore everything else. The ability to read energy dynamics—even before they manifest as a physical phenomenon—can, therefore, be learned by everyone. And since you, as an empath, already have a pronounced sensitivity to subtle energies, you are naturally talented at picking up these skills. So the question is not whether you have psychic powers but what is blocking them!

In my personal experience as a medicine woman, I came to understand that what many underestimate when it comes to developing psychic abilities, such as traveling to other dimensions, seeing auras, doing energy work, etc., is that it's significantly important to look at the unconscious parts of your psyche first. I've learned from studying and practicing shamanic rituals that the veils into other realms are often thinner than we think. The real challenge of mastering psychic powers is to work through everything hidden in the psyche that is clouding our perception. These can be old traumas, beliefs, and predispositions that we carry in our subconscious that prevent our strengths from fully unfolding and bringing truth into the world.

I once had a powerful vision traveling back to a previous incarnation, where I had been a shaman and helped many people with my psychic powers. Yet, in some way, I was no longer present on Earth. I saw my humanity and my own shadows as separate from me; I perceived them as demons that I constantly chased away for peace. I used my light to protect myself and my village from those demons, unaware that I was closing myself off from my own wholeness.

"Demons," as I realized many years later, always find their way as long as they are not integrated. Well camouflaged, they often strike where we are inevitably most connected to Earth: in the family. My brother, another powerful shaman, and I fought each other for a lifetime. He would not accept that I had been appointed shaman of our tribe, so he left our village and started his own tribe. Blind to our history and my traumas, I thought it was his fault alone and that I had no part in the conflict. It was usual for me that powerful people fought each other. This is how it had been for generations.

My brother and I could not make peace within our lifetime. I also failed to give my children the love and attention they needed because that would've required me to be more human. I found it easier to take care of others than my own children. But I pushed this out of my consciousness and told myself that the world needed my service, and therefore, my children had to sacrifice. Those around me also saw me as the great healer with more important things to do than be concerned with the everyday reality of my close relationships. And so my children never complained; they were taught right from the start that this was just how things were. They learned to respect me and that having me as their mother was an honor.

When I got older, I started to withdraw. Wisdom called me, and I followed. I was already very old when I finally dared to take off the glasses of my identification and look at the world with clear eyes. What I saw broke my heart; I saw my children growing into beautiful adults who were deeply wounded at heart. I saw that they were very quiet and closed off to me because they had learned that I wouldn't come whenever they called. I saw how they were very hardened in some places, without mercy, guided by their sometimes closed hearts. I watched them carry on my own wounds and shadows and pass them on to my grandchildren.

I also saw myself and the wounds from my own childhood that I had never dared to look at. I saw the truth that I had brought healing into this world but also a great deal of hurt—driven by shadows I didn't want to see. I had my children called to me to report what I had seen. We cried together, and for the first time, our hearts were truly connected.

Before I died, I made peace with my life and the way I had lived it. Through my deep connection to the sky and spirits, I knew that everything was exactly as it was supposed to be. But now I had also felt the true quality of being well connected to Earth and to the human level of reality. I realized that I and most shamans I knew didn't unify this paradox. We did not know the truth of Earth, we just spoke Heaven's truth. At that moment, I realized how much stronger my psychic abilities could have been and how much more healing they could've brought into the world if I had spent less energy on suppressing my shadows and demons during that lifetime and more energy on connecting to those around me and myself on a human level.

And so I closed my eyes and felt a deep joy well up in me. A deep joy about the coming life that I could already sense. A life that would teach me to live this paradox fully. It would train me to combine the ancient knowledge of Heaven with the ancient knowledge of Earth. It would allow me to learn to unite the light and the dark in my heart. Peacefully and grateful, I said goodbye to my life, and the last breath escaped my body. Silence.

Then, a deep inhale. And here I was, Sanyana—in a different world yet the same. And I knew what I came here for and what I wanted to bring into this time. Joy and gratitude flooded through me, and a deep understanding of my life and why I chose to live it. This is my story, and so I am writing this book today in the hope that it will unite Heaven and Earth, light and darkness, psychic abilities, and humanity. I wish to remind you of all that you are and how to unleash your full potential.

Through my specialization in trauma and shadow work, I could experience firsthand how much more powerful my abilities became through working with instead of against my own humanity; that only when you've met and integrated your deepest shadows and soul pain can your true abilities flourish unhindered and in a way that's aligned with the highest good of all.

In the following chapters, we will explore what subconscious shadows are and how they can block your psychic energies. For example, suppose you have a problem with speaking up for yourself. In that case, this shadow will block the energy flow of your throat chakra, your ability to hear the truth and channel it, and therefore block your clairaudient abilities. Or you might carry a wound of feeling rejected for being too different from others, and your subconscious shadow, therefore, longs to blend in to be accepted. In that case, you might be subconsciously suppressing your abilities or be fearful of them since they might isolate you from others. Whatever the case, this book will help you uncover these and other shadows that might be blocking your full potential and will show you how you can integrate them best to free your hidden gifts.

In the following pages, you will find a collection of powerful exercises, meditations, and food for thought that you can use to get to know and develop your gifts. These techniques are time-proven through my work with clients.

I'm not asking you to believe me. Instead, I want to allow you to experience it for yourself! By the end of this book, you will know what it means to be an empath, how to work with your own traumas, how to unleash your psychic gifts, and how to use your energy to heal yourself and your surroundings. It will take work, lure you out of your comfort zone, and invite you to take a leap into the mysterious here and there to open yourself up to what you previously thought was impossible. But I can tell you one thing: it will be worth it. Because every day, you will get to know yourself (and your true greatness) a little better. Every day, you can write a new chapter in your personal love story. The love story with yourself and life. Because when life becomes an adventure, and you become the hero of your own story, how could you not fall in love?

So, shall we start?

DISCLAIMER

Before we jump into our topic, it is important to note that this book does not make any claim to be scientifically correct. Even though my teachings are in core agreement with today's science, as a spiritual teacher with a strong intuitive connection, I channel both ancient and new knowledge that sometimes does not agree with definitions already established by society.

Especially for terms such as 'empath,' 'trauma', and 'healing,' there exist many inconsistencies in definitions. These can quickly lead to confusion when you start to inform yourself. Both in literature and on the internet, many authors contradict each other. But I don't always feel that one definition is right and the other is wrong. The most important factor for me is whether a concept is coherent and helps me advance my knowledge. So, I would like to share my personal perspective with you, which has arisen from my own experience and years of working with my clients.

The best concepts lead us to recognize ourselves and the world around us on a more profound level and later, after internalization, invite us to discard them again. After all, no concept in this world can even come close to fully describing every aspect of our unique reality. Our true nature is too complex for words.

This also goes for my teachings: I can be an expert in a certain field, and in that role, I am writing this book. But I can never be an expert in "being you." That is your position!

In this world, you might find contradictory and conflicting truths everywhere. This does not mean that one truth is less true than the other. Both are true, but for different people and in different moments or stages of life. You might find a truth that you have never heard before, that no one else could ever point out to you: because it's your very own truth of this moment. So, every time you're presented with new information and techniques, I urge you to continuously ask yourself: "What is true for me? What do I need right now?"

As an empath, it is especially important to always reflect on what your inner voice tells you since you likely struggle or have struggled with seeing and owning your own truth instead of taking on the truth of others. I invite you to let yourself be inspired by external sources but, above all, to reawaken your inner guidance and wisdom. Be curious and explore what's best for yourself. You will become the conscious expert of being yourself by trying yourself out with pleasure. Dare to be creative.

And so, with every exercise in this book, I invite you to feel into yourself and question continuously: Does this feel right for me? Maybe you can even find individual variations of these exercises that touch you even deeper. Then do so! This will strengthen the connection to your own intuition immensely.

My general recommendation for working with this book is to use your own discernment in deciding which exercises you'd like to try and which you'd like to skip or leave out. You might just want to read them and see if you feel inspired to put them into practice, and that is the absolute best approach. To benefit from this book, you don't have to do any exercises at all. Just reading through the suggestions will plant seeds in your mind that are ready to germinate whenever your intuition tells you the time is ripe.

However, the exercises are, of course, highly potent, and by choosing one that you repeat for 5–10 minutes a day, you will see transformation fairly quickly. If 10 minutes a day feels hard at first, try 1 minute! It can be easy! And if it feels easy and you enjoy it, you will automatically increase duration and intensity because your system, deep down, notices how beneficial the exercise is and then naturally wants more. And suddenly, you expand with utmost ease.

This book is structured in a way that will take you on an adventurous journey through the depths of your own shadow pain to uncover unhealed blockages and unleash all the magic and power lying dormant within you. However, you can always jump to a certain chapter first if you feel drawn to do so. All of the exercises mentioned and described in the book can be found in our exercise overview at the beginning of this book.

I also want to strongly encourage you to seek professional guidance and help if you feel like you need it or are experiencing symptoms of dissociation, panic attacks, anxiety, depression, or psychological overwhelm.

Many empaths are used to feeling more intensely than others, and even though—when directed and trained properly, as we will discuss—this can be a great gift, it also can lead many empaths to burn out and leave them prone to develop serious depression and other mental health conditions. So, never hesitate to seek out help sooner rather than later! This doesn't always need to be a psychologist; help can also come from coaches, energy workers, or any other person you trust. The most important thing is that you feel safe and comfortable with this person.

We are here to heal each other and walk the path together. This makes the path easier and more joyful. Some of the exercises in this book go very deep. Please trust yourself if you feel that something is too much or too early for you or if you only want to do it with support. Always listen to your intuition here!

So, with that being said, let's go and take a deep dive into your truth!

BEING AN EMPATH

*a*s a shamanic trauma coach and empath myself, I have been blessed to experience the gift and challenges of this calling both in my own journey as well as in my work with clients. I know it can feel lonely sometimes, and you might've felt misunderstood in the past and maybe even struggled to understand yourself. So, this first chapter is dedicated to looking at the most common signs of being an empath to help you recognize all the different gifts you have been blessed with.

YOU'RE NOT TOO SENSITIVE – YOU HAVE A SUPERPOWER!

When it comes to understanding and developing superpowers, we live in truly remarkable times, where we not only have access to the long-lost or kept information of many shamanic and spiritual traditions, but we also have the science to track tangible phenomena. For a long time, psychic experiences have been seen as hallucinations by those who weren't sensitive enough to perceive them. And as a highly intuitive person, you might've often questioned your own perception. But I am here to tell you that whatever you perceive is very valid. You're not hallucinating, you're not imagining things, and you're not "overly" sensitive; you just have a talent for picking up subtle energies.

So, what does it mean to be an empath? In the most general sense, empaths are seen as those who practice empathy or have a particularly empathic nature. Empathy is officially defined as "the ability to understand and share the feelings of another." It's a form of sensitivity for the sentiments of others; someone with great empathy perceives the experiences of those around firsthand as if they were in that person's place. But how is that possible?

Like any other energy in this universe, much like radio waves, human emotions, and thoughts exist on a vibrational frequency and can be downloaded by anyone open to perceiving them. Technically, this sensitivity is a skill that any human can attain. To empaths, it comes naturally; they oftentimes have learned to read the emotions and feelings of a room at an early age, which opened them up to perceive subtle energies in general.

Modern science is slowly catching up with what shamans have talked about forever, and that is that our universe is composed of energy vibrating at a certain frequency. The world of material phenomena that we perceive through our five senses is actually only a tiny fraction of all the energy information that surrounds us at any time. And our 3D-material world is not the only world that is perceivable. Depending on which frequency you are tuned into, you can tap into different realms that exist simultaneously. It's even possible to be tuned into different dimensions simultaneously.

Throughout history and many different cultures and traditions, those with the gift of tuning into other realms that exist beyond the physical were called shamans and trained to master and safely use their gift to help their village as healers, advisors, and medicine people. They commonly communicated with ancestors or spirits and reported what they read in people's energy fields. The word shaman is age-old and was initially translated as 'someone who sees in the dark.'

They were superheroes because their whole village could count on their guidance and assistance in difficult times—individually and as a unit. They were honored for their dedication to their calling and respected for their inherent need for solitude and meditation. It's not surprising, therefore, that the shamanic traditions seem to understand the sensitivity of an empath who feels beyond the physical, much better than modern science so far can. And not only that, it also holds a few very useful pieces of advice to help you navigate your ability.

Unfortunately, sensitivity is still regarded as a weakness by many in our modern-day society, which surely couldn't be further from the truth. Being an empath often means being misunderstood. In a rational world where feelings often don't weigh as heavy as "hard logical facts," it can be incredibly difficult for the empath to feel seen and acknowledged for all their strengths. I will clearly and logically show you why being sensitive takes incredible strength and what gifts it holds. We'll also look into how you can gain sharp confidence around your superpower.

In sharing my experience, I intend to help you understand yourself better and remember the true power and strength that you have! So, let's start by looking deeper at what it means to be an empath.

TEN UNMISTAKABLE SIGNS OF AN EMPATH

To get a clear idea of what we're talking about, let's start by looking at ten common traits you most likely experience as an empath, as well as some shamanic advice on how to best navigate them.

1. TAKES ON EMOTIONS, FEELINGS, AND THOUGHTS OF THE PEOPLE AROUND

The most common trait of empaths is their innate ability to perceive other people's feelings without even trying. While this can be super useful when trained and perfected, this ability often appears challenging for many empaths before it becomes a blessing. Usually, the empath doesn't notice that it's someone else's sentiment; they pick it up and confuse it with their own. And even if they do recognize it's someone else's energy, they might not know what to do about it if the person themselves is unaware. Due to their openness, empaths easily pick up on the emotions and thoughts of other people. Additionally, empaths often experience emotions in an intensified way compared to non-empaths. Due to their sensitivity, the energies they perceive might seem very "loud" and difficult to ignore.

If you haven't yet mastered holding intense emotions, you might tend to avoid social situations altogether because it can feel draining to be around people. You might experience confusion about your emotional state after a meeting. Maybe you felt exceptionally good when entering the meeting but left feeling sad or frustrated and wondering where the sudden mood change came from. The following exercise will help you distinguish clearly what's yours and what isn't and become more confident in your ability while being around people. The goal in working with this ability is to get to a state where it will be your own choice whether you take on others' emotions or not.

EXERCISE: MEDITATION TO DIFFERENTIATE EMOTIONS

Find a quiet corner where you won't be disturbed for 15 minutes. Breathe, come into your center, and listen to the stillness for a moment. Now, focus on the sensation of the emotion you'd like to examine. Sit with it, feel it, and calmly ask to be shown the origin of that emotion. Don't try to look for it; just let the emotion speak to you and listen. The more often you do this in situations of doubt, the easier you will recognize what is and isn't yours.

2. SENSITIVE TO THE SUFFERING OF OTHERS

The next major trait of empaths is their extreme discomfort in seeing other beings suffer. It's like torture to them. For example, as an empath, you might feel like you are particularly sensitive to any form of violence in your surroundings. Movies and documentaries about violence that might be entertaining or informative to others can leave you deeply traumatized by being confronted with the depiction of agony and pain.

But this is not to be seen as a weakness. On the contrary, it shows how open your heart is and the level of compassion it can hold. The secret to resilience lies in learning to hold intense emotions and letting them wash through you like waves instead of dwelling on them in the aftermath. The more you open up to that natural flow of feelings and energies, the more you will uncover the beauty of this gift, which is feeling deeply connected and helping people feel less lonely in their pain. It doesn't have to be difficult to sense other people's suffering, but it can be fulfilling to be there for them when you are grounded in your inner peace.

But of course, there will be situations in which you don't feel the resources to hold someone else's pain because you aren't grounded enough or because it concerns a movie scene. In those cases, you need to know that you can protect yourself to prevent unwanted energies from penetrating your own energy field. You have that power, too! If you, for whatever reason, are in need of immediate protection, you will find tips on that in Chapter 5.

EXERCISE: FLUSHING OUT OLD AND THIRD-PARTY EMOTIONS

Whenever you find yourself overwhelmed with intense emotions, you can use bodywork to release them. This prevents them from getting stuck in your energy field and body. Movement will help you to stay out of freeze and overwhelm modus. All types of physical movement can help you to free up stuck emotions. This can be through dancing it out, shaking, doing yoga, exercising, running, or even tapping and massaging your body. So whenever there is an old emotion you cannot quite pinpoint but want to let go of, take some time to meditate on that recurring emotion and interrogate it until it reveals itself to you. Then, feel where in your body it is sitting, get moving while breathing deeply into the sensation, and watch the emotion flush out of your system while you do it.

3. PEOPLE TEND TO CONFIDE IN THEM EASILY

Another very typical sign of being an empath is that people feel especially comfortable in their presence and seek their advice regularly. You might be the kind of person strangers confess their secrets to while waiting for the bus or the one friend and family member everybody likes to share their problems with. You are naturally a good listener, and people feel especially understood by you. Others seem to trust you easily, even with their deepest concerns and secrets.

This is likely because of your open aura. People can sense your ability to empathize and may have experienced it before. You intuitively ask the right questions to help people open up, and they can tell that you honestly care. This makes people feel comfortable, safe, and welcome in your presence. Some might even feel like they can recharge in your energy field. You're likely familiar with situations where people seem to crave your energy because it makes them feel good.

The potential problem with this dynamic is when you feel empty and depleted afterward. In the following chapters, we will take a deep look into how you can hold space for yourself and others without feeling depleted and how you can, therefore, become an empowered empath.

4. ABILITY TO 'READ PEOPLE'

As an empath, you might also notice that people tend to feel like you're reading their thoughts or speaking from their soul because they feel so deeply understood in your presence. And that's because you listen more deeply, not only with your human ears or intellect but with your whole being. Since empaths perceive subtle vibrational energy, they often get insights into subtle energy communication between beings at all times.

You might intuitively see into the mental, emotional, or spiritual state of others, which will oftentimes enable you to understand others' deepest intentions, fears, and desires. It's like you are perceiving their core. That way, you can easily turn into a human lie detector once you're aware and in full control of your abilities. Your inner truth sensor will increase immensely by using our meditations and exercises to unlock your psychic abilities since those abilities are nothing more than skills to read and perceive subtle energies in a clear way, as we will explore later.

5. HIGHLY SENSITIVE TO SENSORY STIMULI

Since empaths perceive subtle energy, they are super sensitive to general sensory stimuli. You probably have a tendency to shy away from spending too much time in noisy and busy environments. Since the nervous system of empaths is very fine-tuned and much more excitable than in non-empaths, it quickly registers any change in an environment and gets easily overstimulated or overwhelmed.

Loud sounds and bright lights might bother you more than others, and you'll likely feel uncomfortable around intense stimuli over a long period of time or need more time to recharge afterward. Since empaths are constantly reading the energy surrounding them, they can easily feel overloaded when they are around big gatherings, especially when they are next to people who carry heavy energy.

A person who carries this trait of high sensitivity is commonly referred to as a highly sensitive person by conventional psychology. It's said to be a mostly genetic trait that can be passed on to younger generations and intensified by a dysfunctional home in early childhood. Most empaths have this trait, while not all highly sensitive people develop to become empaths—because empathy is much like the psychic extension of being highly sensitive. From a shamanic perspective, this sensitivity is the seed that enables you to see behind the visible world and experience an extraordinary depth of life.

If this is you, you will greatly benefit from learning to center yourself in your own energy and ground yourself, as we will discuss in the following chapters.

6. PHYSICAL SENSITIVITIES TO TOXINS

Because the empath system is hypersensitive to outside influences, it is much quicker to register negative energies in the environment, such as environmental toxins or old emotions that are stored in the body and is also much quicker to react to them. This manifests on a physical level as well.

Especially in environments where the empath experiences heavy emotions while being restricted in expressing them, they might find their immune system declining with time. This can show up as getting sick often or even as mental health conditions. You might also generally be more sensitive to substances such as plant medicine and caffeine. A healthy body is the foundation of your work as an energy healer, so it is crucial for every empath to detox regularly.

For this reason, I recommend getting your body to sweat, be it in a shamanic sweat lodge, the sauna, or through exercise. Move your body in whatever way is pleasurable to you. By drinking plenty of fresh alkaline water and eating a diet that is suitable for your body, you create the best possible conditions for your psychic abilities to flourish and for your human suit to bloom into its full strength. Take notice of what nourishes your mind, body, and soul, and make sure you ingest things with gratitude, filling your cells with love. Oftentimes, the how is much more important than the what. Remember that your body is your most sophisticated tool during your stay on Earth and should be cared for with love.

7. ANXIOUS AND EASILY STRESSED OUT

With a hypersensitive nervous system, most empaths are always alert to detect the harmony levels of their surroundings. This means that your nervous system has a lot to process and, therefore, gets stressed more quickly. Situations that might not bother others can feel nerve-racking, even if you don't necessarily show it externally. This is the reason why empaths tend to burn out more often than non-empaths and suffer more often from anxiety.

But it's not only that empaths are more sensitive; they also sense what's out of balance in the world around them, which can be quite overwhelming at times. There is value in acknowledging what kind of world we live in and that being exhausted by some things can be a good sign! Or as Jiddu Krishnamurti said: "It is no measure of health to be well adjusted to a profoundly sick society."

So while grounding and centering techniques—as we will discuss later—

can help you to calm yourself and replace anxiety with a feeling of strength and empowerment, it is equally important to learn to create an environment that is as stress-free as possible and to learn not to expose oneself to certain energies. Another powerful tool on your way to build that environment is calling in a spirit animal for support.

EXERCISE: CALLING IN YOUR SPIRIT ANIMAL

To start, find a quiet spot and take a few deep breaths. Let yourself sink and relax deeply. Once you are connected to your breath, contemplate the question: Which animal radiates the most power, calm, and security for me? Now, invoke the spirit of this animal by inviting it to join you. Visualize this animal coming toward you and connecting with you. Notice how it radiates all the qualities you need in your present situation. Know that from now on, your spirit animal will always be with you, reassuring you that everything will be fine. Your spirit animal is your secret bodyguard.

Visualize a bright light band connecting you and your spirit animal, and let it become stronger and stronger with every breath. How does this encounter make you feel? When you open your eyes, continue to imagine that your spirit animal is next to you. It will always be here with you and will accompany you. All it takes is for you to open yourself to perceive it. For example, imagine how your spirit animal walks next to you and how supported that makes you feel when going for a walk.

Over time, you will strengthen your relationship with your spirit animal and feel more and more confident about your backup, even in stressful situations. You know you can always call upon your bodyguard by imagining it standing in front of you and around you to protect and provide strength. Sometimes, your spirit animal might even put their head on your pelvis to remind you to relax, or it might put its head on your heart to let love flow into you and remind you that you are not alone. This exercise alone can transform your whole life because you will experience new strength and security with your spirit animal at your side.

8. NEEDS ALONE TIME TO RECHARGE

Empaths generally have an introverted side to them and seek alone time to recharge. Since there is a constant overload of sensory information around others, empaths usually withdraw whenever they feel tired and crave to be in their own energy. Living in a world that's quite fast, loud, and unempathetic might fatigue you easily, and you might even feel like you need more sleep than others to feel rested, and that is perfectly normal.

Since your brain and energy system are working through a lot of sensory and extrasensory information during the day, they have a lot to process at night and, therefore, need quite a bit of extra rest. So, the extra nap in the afternoon or the extra couple of hours in the morning are a beautiful gift you're invited to give yourself to embrace the hard work your system is doing.

You might also like to take things a little slower compared to your peers, and that's where a beautiful gift lies—the gift to perceive everything more deeply. That you recharge in your own presence speaks for your deep bond with yourself and your intuition and that you know how to fill your own cup whenever you have to. The exercise below can be additional to refill your batteries and connect you to the infinite source of energy we all get access to when we turn our attention inside.

EXERCISE: USING A MANTRA TO RECHARGE

Whenever you feel low in energy or depleted, take a moment to repeat your favorite mantra. This can be in a dramatic chant with background music or silently in meditation, depending on what works best for you in a situation. Choose a mantra that connects you right to the divine spirit and feel how it replenishes your being with source frequency and unconditional love. This will help you clear out any unwanted energies and get stagnancy back into the flow. Whatever comes up during the mantra meditation, let it flow out, feel it, and let it wash you back into peace.

Note: You will find a playlist with our favorite mantras in our Spotify bundle.

9. SENSITIVE TO SPIRIT AND SYNCHRONICITIES

Because of the empath's innate sensitivities to perceive subtle energy, they usually have an easy time connecting to spirits and divine energies, which are subtle in nature. By being open to perceiving them, empaths oftentimes become powerful magnets to divine vibrations and naturally attract synchronicities. This could be displayed as frequent coincidental luck, a gift to channel higher wisdom and spirit guides, an intuitive connection to animals and nature, or inspired creativity. This predisposition makes empaths excellent students for spiritual practices.

You will notice that the more you communicate with the Universe and the spirits around you, the more they will respond and blow your mind. You might find yourself getting unexpected support for a problem that has given you a serious headache before. Things might start to work out in your favor in miraculous ways, and you might start seeing repeating numbers such as 111, 222, or 123. Whenever that happens, you know the divine energies are working for you behind the scenes. Meditation is a crucial practice to open yourself up to this kind of communication and learn to listen to divine guidance. The following exercise can help you establish a solid connection to spirit and invite more synchronicities into your life.

EXERCISE: CONNECT TO YOUR DIVINE GUIDANCE

If you feel inspired, you can create an altar for this exercise on which you place objects or pictures that remind you of your connection to the divine— whatever that means to you. Activate the altar by lighting a candle and performing an opening ritual. For example, with the words: "I invite all energies and spirits that are well disposed toward me to support me and be here with me." Or "I ask for connection to the highest and invite the divine soul of all beings." You can either say them in your mind or say it out loud. You can also invite a very specific force that you intuitively feel you want by your side, such as archetypes like Mary Magdalene, Jesus, Kali, Isis, or whoever resonates with you.

You can ask if there is any important information for you to receive right now or just bathe yourself in the connection and light of the energies you invited. Once you're done, thank the energies you've been connecting with and close the portal by blowing out the candle. You'll be surprised how quickly magic moves into your lives once you open the doors to the divine!

Create a daily meditation habit to connect to your divine guidance on a regular basis. Give this as much priority as the relationship with your highest divine allies deserves. You may start with 5 to 10 minutes and increase the time however suits you best.

Note: If you want to complement this practice with meditation music, we have a beautiful playlist for this purpose in our Spotify bundle.

10. FEELS INTENSE EMOTIONS

Another major sign of being an empath and a huge reason why so many empaths feel misunderstood is their increased sensitivity with which they experience emotions. It's like empaths perceive everything at full volume. So when they express their sentiments to others, they're often perceived as extra or too dramatic. This leads many empaths to feel uncomfortable with expressing their feelings authentically or dismissing the emotions in the first place.

And since empaths generally process a huge load of different emotions, both their own and those of others, they can easily get overwhelmed by the weight of sorrow and feel like they are drowning in grief, burning in anger, or freezing in fear. Dealing with emotions could very likely be the biggest challenge for many empaths because they likely never learned how to properly deal with them. So, let's take a look at healthy ways to process and release intense feelings.

HOW TO NAVIGATE INTENSE EMOTIONS

The first important step in navigating intense emotions is taking on a proper perspective toward them. As someone who feels intensely, you might tend to consider emotions a burden because they are hard to control, and you might feel overwhelmed by them often. I want to help you discover the beauty behind those experiences and how you can reap the secret boons they hold.

They are beautiful gifts that invite you to experience a situation on a deeper dimension, with all the intensity it holds, and the more you can allow them to flow through you, the more alive they will make you feel. To become an empowered empath, it's essential for you to accept your nature and the fact that you feel intensely, and you will have to express and release those feelings regularly to stay connected with yourself.

You'll be surprised how deep and dark emotions often reveal experiences of freedom and bliss once they're properly felt. And that's because they are much like clouds that pass in a clear blue sky. The clear blue sky is your true nature, which exists in blissful serenity underlying every heavy feeling that passes by. Once you are fully relaxed in the blue sky, you might even appreciate the clouds for their beautiful play and get excited about the adventure they announce.

Emotions are messengers, direct feedback on how your system evaluates a certain situation, thought, or memory. When you find yourself in a situation that is in harmony with your being and your ideals, your emotional body will produce vibrations of comfort and joy. When something inspires you, you might feel a rush of excitement and bliss. And if your environment throws you off balance or appears hostile in any way, you might experience feelings of grief or anger.

Emotions are the pulsating aliveness that runs through your being in the form of clear signals. Oftentimes, arising emotions feel like too much to handle, and we refuse to feel them through, but instead, we repress those feelings by distracting or numbing ourselves. In that case, the emotion gets stored in our body as an unfinished process and waits there for the next opportunity to be expressed. When that happens, our subconscious starts creating and attracting scenarios that seem familiar to the one that originally triggered the emotions. Whenever we find a similar situation while still carrying those unlived emotions, we get the chance to relive and release them. When you get out of a situation that triggered you, and you notice this emotion lingering around long after you've left the situation, it is always a hint that old emotions are stored in your field.

The more you feel, the more you heal. Because the more you allow your emotions to flow through, the more they get released from your system, the lighter you will feel, and the more space is cleared up for new experiences. Whenever you surrender to the flow of emotions, they will guide you to understand yourself on a deeper level. Sometimes, they might reveal an old story or memory you've long forgotten. This is always an opportunity to listen and hear your body out.

Emotions can be our greatest teachers if we allow them to be. Anger shows us where our boundaries are being violated both by ourselves and others. It shows us when we're going astray from our truth and need to adjust our direction. It gives us the strength to stand up for ourselves and our beliefs.

Fear shows us where we're not yet at peace and can learn to surrender to the higher power behind the universe. It challenges us to take a larger perspective, face our own limitations, and shows us where we can rise above ourselves. Through fear, we learn what courage means.

Guilt shows us where we cannot yet see our human innocence and where it is time to love ourselves even more. Shame shows us that we have been conditioned in the past by society and our environment and need to free ourselves from these limitations. I can tell you at this point that there is nothing worth being ashamed of.

Shame shows us where it's time to challenge learned assumptions. Shame and guilt keep us small through the crazy concept that we have to be perfect. But in the end, one truth remains: we are all human, and by taking a closer look, we realize that we all carry the same "flaws." And that's okay. As humans, we can allow ourselves to be perfectly imperfect.

Grief and sadness teach us compassion about the pains that come with being human. They offer to open your heart and heal it. Cleanse it from all the heaviness, panic, numbness, helplessness, and desperations of life on this planet. It cleanses you and flushes out everything that is stuck, uncovering a core of unconditional self-love and love for others.

Jealousy and envy point us toward our true potential, which we haven't yet admitted. They show us where we don't fully appreciate ourselves and allow us to be who we truly desire to be.

All these emotions are a deep connection with your human experience, and once you learn to flow with them, you will receive their deep gifts. So, even if you might shy away from surrendering to those intense emotions, learning how to navigate them and reap the full benefit is absolutely worth it! As an empath, you are gifted with the ability to feel deeply, and once you recognize the wonder behind that ability, you'll discover more and more gifts behind every emotion.

EXERCISE: RIDING DIFFICULT EMOTIONS LIKE WAVES

The secret to navigating intense emotions lies in learning to ride emotions like waves, without drowning in them, by reminding yourself that whatever emotion you're facing, however intense and overwhelming it might appear, it is only temporary! Much like a wave, it will slowly build up to a peak and then subside. Let it wash through you without clinging to it. "It will pass" or "This too shall pass" can be useful affirmations to repeat in those moments when you feel overwhelmed.

The more you surrender to the feeling and fully accept it at that moment, the quicker it will be released from your system. It can help tremendously to just name the emotion you are experiencing, thereby acknowledging it, and then lovingly talk yourself through opening up. Comfort yourself by saying things like: "It's okay, you are safe. You can open up to feel through this sadness," or "It's alright, I got you."

Gently remind yourself that every emotion happens in your highest interest as a messenger that can ultimately help you release old baggage and gain more strength and capacity to hold emotions with grace both for yourself and others. Try to find the hidden boons behind the experience. What were you able to release? What did you learn about yourself?

Acknowledge how alive you felt at the top of this mighty wave. How your whole being was vibrating in the face of this emotion. See the beauty of this raw and authentic human experience. Visualize how every one of these realizations strengthens your sense of stability on your surfboard until, with patience and practice, you reach a sense of peace and serenity, even in the middle of the mightiest tsunami.

For this exercise, put on supportive music to find the right flow and hop onto the wave. Write down all thoughts that might arise in you and note what they trigger within yourself. Once you're done, you might read your own words and again observe how they make you feel. Tell yourself what's on your chest or tell it to someone who is just there to listen without making too many comments about what is being said.

Try to express yourself from the feeling perspective and not from the mind. Allow everything to flow out freely. No matter how crazy it might sound, this is not about making sense. You can allow yourself to authentically express how you feel. Cry, scream, laugh, vocalize, and shake yourself, whatever helps to release as much emotion as possible.

I also want to note that sometimes you might feel the movement is counterproductive because you'd risk losing control of the emotion and could do harm to yourself or others. Anger is an excellent example of that even though it can be super healing to scream at the top of your lungs and hit passionately into a pillow, in some situations, you might notice your anger getting out of hand and too much to hold by yourself. In those cases, become as still as possible and breathe through the emotion. Allow that anger to expand in your chest until it bursts your heart wide open and reveals the deep sorrow and helplessness underlying it.

If you feel panic arising at any point during the exercise, you can regulate yourself by bringing your awareness to your body. Give yourself a tight hug and remind yourself that all is well in this present moment. Become aware of your surroundings and breathe deeply and slowly with prolonged exhalation until you feel safe in your body again. Then, examine what beliefs are underlying the previous panic. If holding yourself is too difficult or overwhelming for you, consider calling in a spirit animal or divine support, as already discussed in previous exercises. Let these energies hold you and breathe with you. You can do it! And you are worth it!

Working through these intense emotions and experiences takes courage and resilience, and you have my deepest respect for the hard work you do in feeling for yourself and with those around you. Every time you surrender to feel through an intense emotion, you increase your capacity to hold these energy waves. This is a gift that is desperately needed in our world, which is full of so many suppressed emotions. This is why you, my dear empath, are not too sensitive. You are a superhero!

THE EMPATH'S SHADOW

*M*uch like our empathy, our psychic senses are abilities that are inherent in us as human beings and that we can always remember and use. When it comes to unlocking them, it is important that we first look at our traumas and shadows, as these can often either completely block our perception or cause us to misinterpret the information we receive.

This is because unprocessed trauma can cause us to see the world through past experiences, so our interpretation of this information can be clouded. Another reason to address trauma and its resulting shadows is that those often require a lot of energy when running in the background, which can be quite draining to our energy field. They sit in our psyche as unre-solved baggage in the form of emotions that want to be seen and dealt with.

Therefore, to perceive the truth of things and to unleash the full power of our psychic abilities, we must be aware of our wounds and shadows so that they no longer cloud our perception and weaken our powers. To be in connection with our shadows and wounds also carries the power to ground our psychic abilities in this world, connecting them with our humanity and thereby establishing true balance within us.

WHAT IS THE SHADOW?

Shadow is a term commonly used in psychology and refers to unconscious behaviors that often arise from an experienced trauma. Trauma refers to specific negative experiences that have overwhelmed our system and left a mark on our psyche. Out of this mark emerged a specific unconscious pat-tern of behavior to prevent the repetition of the traumatic experience. A shadow is born.

To make this even more comprehensible: A good example of a typical empath shadow that blocks psychic perception would be mistrusting one's own intuition. Like most empaths, you might've forgotten how to hear and trust your intuition in the past because you were repeatedly told your per-ception was inaccurate when growing up, even when, in truth, it was never wrong. It just wasn't acceptable for the people around you.

Many empaths learned early on to disregard their inner voice whenever it conflicted with their environment. Especially as children, we want and need to be accepted by our peers, so the trauma of rejection can lead the empath to desensitize themselves to their inner guidance.

If that is the case for you, the first step to reconnect to your intuition should be to step into your unconscious patterns, find out why your system is blocking your inner voice, integrate it into your conscious perception, and release the old mechanism.

And the same goes for all psychic perception, which we are technically all born with but unlearn and suppress into the depth of our unconscious mind. If we habitually ignore a certain trait of ourselves because it is uncomfortable to acknowledge, we're ashamed of it, or are simply convinced we don't have that trait, it will disappear from our perception. It's not visible and, therefore, hidden from the field of awareness. It's in the dark. These habits that we've formed in the past to turn a blind eye to certain things or behave in ways that don't match our true selves we call "shadows." In fact, there might be a complete alternative personality within you, comprising everything you don't acknowledge about yourself.

As explained earlier, another reason to work through your shadow is that if you have many unconscious mental processes running in the background, it can drain your energy field and make it difficult to be receptive to high vibrational energy. We often have to let go of old baggage to create space for the new.

For example, a people pleaser shadow might get triggered and might have you stay in a situation when your intuition is actually telling you to leave. Or you might not speak up for yourself when someone crosses your boundaries, and this betrayal in your own integrity weakens your confidence, and energy starts leaking. Or someone might act as if you weren't good enough and trigger a sense of guilt. You might later feel depleted, as if that person stole your energy, but really, the guilt could only get triggered because there was already an underlying feeling of unworthiness present in you.

Once you realize there is a shadow of things you don't consciously acknowledge within yourself and your surroundings, you'll start to see how this blind spot is precisely what hinders your psychic awareness from expanding. By bringing that shadow into the light of your own consciousness, you will return to a state of wholeness where you are able to access your full power.

In my experience, this is why one very powerful tool to unleash your psychic gifts is to work with your shadow and understand your subconscious processes. You may be surprised at all the abilities and personality traits hidden within you. And even though shadow work can sound scary at times, it is actually quite exciting because it's not only past pains and traumas we will discover as we take a step into the unconscious part of our being.

Our shadow also holds all the unconscious potentials that we learned to suppress due to certain expectations that either our friends, family, or the society we grew up in imposed on us. All the suppressed gifts and talents that were too loud, too unconventional, too wild, too controversial, too free, too daring, or too confronting for your environment and that you learned to suppress also lay dormant here.

You might, for example, consider yourself a quiet person, but when you take a closer look, have you really always been quiet? Were you allowed to be loud as a child? Or could it be possible that you experienced caretakers who didn't like to hear very much from you when you were growing up?

Discovering your own shadow could very possibly turn out to be the greatest adventure of your life because working with your shadow can lead you to discover all the possibilities that lie buried under unhealed trauma and outdated beliefs. The trauma might be long in the past, but the protective mechanism still runs how you navigate the world.

As long as the shadow is unconscious, it keeps you from embodying and being your true self, including many of your biggest strengths and gifts. To unlock the full potential of your being, you'll need to understand and integrate those hidden parts of yourself and shine awareness onto any subconscious habits that might be self-sabotaging or hindering your soul's evolution.

In the next chapter, we will look at some of the most common core wounds and traumas many empaths carry, as well as the resulting shadows that typically disconnect empaths from their psychic perception.

THE NATURE OF TRAUMA AND THE INNER CHILD

So, what is the nature of trauma? Even though there are many different definitions and perspectives on trauma, what I refer to when I use this word is any event that caused a direct threat or distress to the human system in a way that was overwhelming and left us defenseless.

When we are unable to feel through all the emotions that a situation brings up and can't process the experience in a healthy way, it can alter our consciousness and our body, especially our nervous system. The unprocessed experience is stored as trauma in our system. It shows as a form of constant alertness and anxiety (often unconscious) that the suffered discomfort might reoccur or even as a habitual reliving of the event. Until we finally revisit and integrate the experience and thereby release it. Integration means to become aware of the stored emotion or sensation, to listen to it, and to allow it to express itself. We learn to hold what happened with a capacity and resources that were not available at the time of the initial trauma.

Often, another important point is to cognitively categorize and reframe the experience so that it can find a place in one's personal story that doesn't negatively impact one's worldview anymore. Through this process, core beliefs and experiences like "the world is dangerous" can be changed to "I am present and safe in this very moment. I am resilient, and I embrace the uncertainty of life."

To get a clear understanding of trauma, it is essential to realize that it doesn't require a car accident or a frontline war experience to create this type of severe distress for a human being. We are highly sensitive creatures, and especially in our early childhood years, we don't have much capacity to endure discomfort. Particularly, the behavior of our loved ones during those years can create lasting traumatic impressions in our system.

For children who cannot yet regulate themselves when working through emotions, situations like being punished or left crying alone feel like torture. And even as adults, we oftentimes take on trauma in overwhelming situations. Trauma can be defined as anything that subjectively feels too much, too fast, too soon, too much for too long, or not enough for too long.

Since the human system is designed to constantly adapt and thereby prevent future damage, it creates and adapts automated defenses to those traumatic events that are meant to ensure that an already experienced distress won't happen again—this is the so-called trauma response. So after trauma, the system often stays on alert, always ready to prevent the suffered agony. It adapts to running in survival mode. While this mechanism may save your well-being in a life-or-death situation or seem to prevent future heartbreak, it also takes an incredible amount of energy and eventually drains the system if it doesn't return to relaxation.

Now, since the traumatic event in itself is usually something that the survivor wants to forget or even ignore, it often gets blocked out of our waking consciousness and is eventually forgotten. A pain that is still there, hidden in our subconscious, but that we never look at. It gets stored in the body as information to back up the installed trauma response that is still running in the background. It becomes an automated process that we often don't understand, question, or even notice. It becomes part of our so-called shadow personality.

If a child, for example, learns early on that crying gets them punished because their caretakers react agitated, the system learns to hide true emotions and won't express them in front of other people. As an adult, the memory of being punished might've long faded, but the trauma response became a personality trait. Now, these individuals might struggle to communicate their personal desires and needs to others, which is considered dangerous by their system. They might introduce themselves to new relationship partners as someone who just doesn't show emotions.

Whenever you are doing something without understanding why, it's time to look at your shadows. In your subconscious lies the answer, and in some weird way, it always makes sense. The great paradox is that oftentimes, it is the default mechanism itself that recreates the traumatic scenario because we adapt to be with the exact type of people that traumatized us in the first place.

Someone who has learned in their childhood that it's unsafe to stand up for their own needs and show emotions will later tend to attract people who aren't caring and considerate of their needs. The familiar treatment creates a false sense of safety for our system, even when, in reality, we do desire someone who understands and honors our needs. Psychology commonly sees this mechanism as our natural tendency to seek the familiar and refers to this as trauma bonding.

From a shamanic perspective, what happens in trauma is that a part of the soul, the spark of pure divine consciousness that inhabits the human avatar, leaves the body as it becomes inhabitable for an energy of such high vibration. To prevent the soul from separating completely, which would mean the body's death, the soul splits, and the purest part of it retreats to a safe space, from where it doesn't return on its own. This creates a void in the human being, a feeling of having lost something. According to this theory, by calling back all soul parts, we step into our fully empowered self, which is known as soul retrieval. This is often a lifelong journey, and it is the exact reason your soul came here. To learn and grow. To experience separation and return to wholeness again.

In spirituality and shamanism, it's believed that as adults, we tend to repeat the same painful situations we experienced as children so that we can recognize the pain and heal from it. This pattern is seen as part of our soul's journey. As we become aware of the trauma and understand that we deserve better, we stop repeating these patterns in our external experiences. Through this process, we learn that true security comes from within ourselves. As a result, we start attracting people who are good for us and who understand our needs because we are now doing the same for ourselves.

To release trauma, we first need to bring it to our awareness and then consciously integrate what happened into our system. For this, you want to ensure that you find a safe place where the emotion can be released. This is, of course, something that children cannot do without the proper support of a caretaker, which often didn't exist, so they grow up carrying unhealed wounds and unprocessed old emotional baggage.

And even adults often struggle to fully feel through trauma on their own. We must first learn how to navigate intense emotional charges without losing our inner calm. Therefore, in order to access deeper layers of the original trauma, secure support is initially necessary. In spiritual circles, we often hear the concept that you can find all healing internally, independent of any external support. But sometimes, our system needs to experience being held by another person in order to heal. As an adult, it is important to be aware of this need and respect it.

However, if you currently don't have good support, you can still make significant progress on your own. You can gradually approach and teach your system that it can trust you today and that it is now safe to experience old emotions fully. As explained in the following exercise, becoming aware of your wounds and working lovingly with your inner child will allow your emotions to flow through you and thereby contribute greatly to your wholeness and gradually diminish the power of your shadows. By working with your inner child, you are reparenting your past self and helping your body release stuck emotions.

Another way to heal past trauma is to reconnect with a version of yourself that is pre-trauma and closest to your own soul essence. To find yourself there, you need to go back to the point before the trauma happened and recognize which part of you was lost. Get in contact with that soul part and ask what it needs to come back. You can also go all the way back in your history to the point where your soul was still most complete, usually in your very early childhood or even at the moment right before you entered your mother's womb. There, you can remember your essence and invite it back into your being.

EXERCISE: MEET YOUR INNER CHILD MEDITATION

This meditation is a beautiful way to connect to your inner child and find any core wounds that caused your soul spark to withdraw. Start by finding a comfortable spot where you won't be disturbed, sit down, and connect to your breathing. Have a picture of your own self as a child ready and look at the picture for some time. What do you see when you look at this child? What is the child thinking and feeling? What are their fears and worries? What are their joys?

Now, close your eyes and envision your inner child standing right in front of you. What would you like to say to your younger self? What would you like to ask? Take your time to make contact and get to know your child self as best as possible. This will be your best friend and companion on your path to healing yourself. The better you understand your inner child, the better you'll understand yourself and your own subconscious behaviors and desires. You can use this exercise to address specific wounds in your psyche, as we will in the following pages, or just to spend time and establish a bond with your inner child. This will be the best foundation for any deeper healing sessions.

Note: Find a guided meditation for you and your inner child in our free meditation bundle.

THE EMPATH'S CHILDHOOD

Looking into one's own childhood wounds might be the toughest part of our work on becoming a fully empowered empath. Every childhood experience is unique, not only in the actual circumstances but also in the way the individual perceives it. And since everybody stores a unique set of traumatic memories, every system has a unique set of shadow behaviors resulting from learned trauma responses.

However, we frequently see a common childhood trauma at the root of highly developed empathic skills: neglect and abuse. People who are extremely empathic and tuned into the emotional and mental states of others often develop these skills out of survival reasons, growing up in environments where their well-being depended on reading their caretaker's mood.

For many empaths, this means they grew up around mentally unstable caretakers, often with narcissistic tendencies. What I mean by that is parents who, for example, tended to have low empathy for their children, made them responsible for their own well-being, had extreme mood swings, cared more about their own needs, were controlling or even manipulative, and didn't tolerate their child having an individual opinion. Parents who were neither able to deal with their child's emotions in a healthy way nor regulate their own emotions as helpful role models. When you grow up with a caretaker who treats you differently, depending on their mood, and might suddenly withdraw or even hurt or threaten your safety, you will learn early on to read their moods and figure out how to influence them to your best advantage. Empathy becomes a survival skill and, after time, a default mode. The child then grows up to navigate the world and difficult situations with empathy.

It is important for me to emphasize here that it is not about blaming parents for why we carry certain shadows today. Their behavior was the result of their own childhood trauma, and I am deeply convinced that every person always does their best with the resources they have. In shamanism, we even believe that as a soul, we choose our parents, knowing all the issues they carry and the challenges that will arise from them.

It also does not necessarily mean that you had a bad childhood. Perhaps there was a lot of light in your childhood, which is beautiful. But we have all experienced darkness as well; how could it be otherwise, on this earth and in this polarity? It is important to openly look at and acknowledge these childhood situations of darkness. Not to find blame but to heal ourselves and to truly see our inner child.

The second possible way one grows up to be an empath is not through trauma but by being raised by fully empowered empaths, who pass down their abilities and teach their children by example. This, of course, is the ideal case scenario. An empath raised in love and understanding will naturally feel very inclined with their psychic abilities because they don't have too many shadows suppressing their senses or clouding their energetic perception. While I see this kind of empath upbringing more and more often—which is a wonderful development in our overall collective—the large majority of cases I've witnessed had trauma as a trigger of their empathic skills.

It is on us to enable the next generation of empaths to learn through positive examples. This means the more empaths heal their childhood traumas and become empowered; the more children will get to develop their empathic gifts through love and grow up to be empowered as well. In order to heal, we must become aware of the wound, so here are the three most common childhood traumas I see in empaths.

1. FEELING OF LONELINESS

Loneliness can be a severe issue for empaths and might be the biggest dilemma they face in life. Many might not realize how deep their need for intimacy really is. Since empaths fluidly tune into the feelings of those around them, they develop a strong sense of oneness and connection to others. Especially those who grew up with narcissistic parents, as defined earlier, often weren't treated as independent individuals but rather as belonging or even possession of their parents. A part of themselves, essentially.

This way, empaths learn early on to identify with the needs of others. Sadly, for most empaths who grew up in dysfunctional homes, their resulting longing for oneness with others hasn't been fulfilled but often led to emotional pain through rejection, abandonment, or manipulation.

As adults, they might struggle with feelings of loneliness and betrayal when they notice that the other is not reciprocating the same depth of feeling or when they feel misunderstood, which happens more often than not. Empaths feel deeply, and not being able to share their vulnerable, intense side can leave them feeling desperate for companionship. They may try to suppress this need to protect themselves from being hurt, but they most likely won't be able to keep it up over a long time, as they live for relationships even more than others.

If this trauma remains unhealed, the empath might tend to compensate by fleeing into fantasy worlds or attracting toxic relationships, as will be discussed in the following pages. The eternal longing for connection and oneness is healed by the realization that you are already one with everything, and your gift for empathy is your invitation to experience this truth in a very felt and real way. By activating your heart space, as we will learn in the following chapter, you can find a deep and fulfilling connection to everything that is, reminding you of your inherent wholeness. And from this state of wholeness, you will automatically attract people who reflect that same level of loving fulfillment and have the same strong need for deep, truthful connection as you.

2. LACKING SAFETY IN THE PRESENCE OF OTHERS

The next common wound we often find in empaths is a sense of unsafety when being around people. Since people with these high levels of empathic abilities particularly often come from dysfunctional families, they often didn't learn to feel safe and protected in their surroundings. Maybe their caretaker only provided affection whenever they were having a good day and threw temper tantrums whenever they had a bad day. In those cases, the child learns to always be on the lookout for danger in the form of bad mood episodes whenever in the presence of others. These children learn firsthand how humans tend to project their anger or frustration onto their environment and start to fight it blindly. So, their program learns that people in a bad mood are a threat to one's safety.

And some are, no doubt. But the difference is that you're not a child anymore; now, you are independent and usually capable of protecting yourself or leaving unsafe situations. It's important for your being to fully understand that in most cases as a grown-up, other people's bad moods do not pose a real threat to your safety but rather trigger a learned feeling of discomfort because you haven't learned how to feel safe around angry people or people who disagree with you. This might show up as the underlying anxiety of saying or doing something wrong.

This wound is an invitation to master the ability to stay grounded in yourself. You don't have to make everyone happy to be safe around them. You and your soul are keeping yourself safe. You have the chance to learn how to be centered in yourself and stand firm in your own truth. This is how you stop absorbing other people's energy by filling up your container with your own energy and being centered in your own loving essence.

3. LOST SENSE OF SELF

This is a tricky one. As specialists in understanding people, empaths are extraordinarily good at detecting the perspectives of others and following their personal stories. The problem is that they sometimes get lost in them, taking on the identity of how others see them and forgetting who they truly are. That is because of their unique way of perceiving life.

When taking a closer look, we find that everyone has a certain narrative that runs their life and becomes a lens through which they look at things. Each individual has a unique story, which shapes how they see the world and themselves. By being so highly attuned to understanding others and their stories, empaths easily lose touch with their own story, their own version of events, and their own self-image as soon as they are in the presence of another person.

This habit is oftentimes rooted in childhood experiences of being repeatedly told that one is inadequate and that there's something inherently wrong with the empath's perspective. Especially if they grew up in dysfunctional homes or with caretakers who showed narcissistic tendencies, they might have constantly been forced to adapt to live by the truth of others and disregard their own. This leaves them unable to acknowledge their own perspective of things later in their adult years.

They might feel sudden self-doubt once they notice someone else's judgment of their person and take that judgment as valid feedback. Or they might listen to someone who's a very good speaker and knows how to use emotion to reinforce their point. They will be swamped and carried away by their emotions, finding themselves easily embracing the other one's truth.

Empaths have a particularly hard time staying in their self-image, to the point that most aren't even sure about who they really are underneath. The truth is that most empaths understand other people better than they understand themselves. So, the unconscious empath will very easily take on other people's perspectives as their own. The conscious empath, on the other hand, is not blinded by the emotions of others. They know this may be their counterpart's truth, but it doesn't mean they have to accept it as their own. Instead, they examine what could really be true for them.

So, getting to know yourself and becoming clear in your self-image is by far the most crucial step in becoming an empowered, confident empath. To get there, it is important to spend quality time with yourself. Regularly! Get to know yourself on a deeply personal level. Learn to feel yourself and notice your own emotions as they emerge. Make it a habit of interrogating every emotion that arises and follow its trace all the way to its source, whether that be your own energy body or the story of others.

It's also important to trust what you will find out and honor your own perspective whenever you do spot one of your own emotions. Become clear about what role you want to embody in this life. Whenever you find yourself getting lost in someone else's perspective or in a life situation where someone dictates who you are and projects onto you, you'll focus back on the self-image you perceive from your soul. Don't be surprised if this image turns out to be way bigger than you would have ever imagined. That is the real beauty of getting in contact with your soul. You open the door to a vision that extends our human imagination.

Once you are anchored in your own truth, you can reap the beautiful gift behind this ability to tune into others so deeply: the ability to take on new perspectives and become a translator of dimensions and worldviews with a deep understanding of all the individual perspectives of humans.

EXERCISE: SOUL MEETS TRAUMA MEDITATION

This exercise is another great way to heal past trauma and a valuable addition to your inner child's work. To open your healing space, find a quiet spot where you won't be disturbed and connect to your breathing. Think back to an experience that broke your human heart badly and got stored as trauma in your body. Now, picture yourself walking on the path toward healing. Picture the landscape you're walking in as detailed as possible. Then, watch yourself walk toward your luminous soul right into its arms. The more detailed you experience the scene, the more powerful its effect. Feel the warm care of your soul, see its aura, and hear its loving whisper.

Notice how the warm soul energy holds your pain and stills it like a crying baby who just wants to be taken care of. Cry if you feel like crying. Release everything that comes up at that moment. Scream, chant or sing if that helps you to let go. Laugh or dance if you feel the bliss of healing arising. Realize that even in the deepest pains of human existence, your soul will be there to comfort you. Surrender to what you have always longed for: Being held and loved, no matter what. Feel the unconditional love within your own heart. Repeat this meditation whenever needed.

Note: Find a supportive playlist for this exercise in our free Spotify bundle.

FIVE COMMON SHADOWS OF AN EMPATH

After looking at the common traumas, I want to discuss a few typical shadow behaviors and habits that often result from those early childhood traumas and the gifts that can be discovered when working through them.

1. TENDENCY TO FLEE INTO FANTASY WORLDS

The first common shadow many empaths carry is their habit of mentally escaping uncomfortable situations by withdrawing into their secret mind spaces. Maybe you've observed this in yourself before. As an empath, you likely have a vibrant inner world full of imagination and awe. This world of imagination often becomes the empath's safe space, their last resort, where they are guaranteed to be undisturbed and can create whatever scenario they desire to experience. And there is so much to discover.

Maybe you've been the dreamer in class and were constantly reminded to be present and to focus. Maybe your friends called you out for drifting away during conversations. Or maybe you just loved to get lost in books and movies for hours and hours and started to enjoy it even more than your real life. What many empaths don't know is that their habit of withdrawing into fantasy worlds is often a protective mechanism of their system that resulted from a lack of safety in their childhood.

In their fictional worlds, empaths can distract themselves from the heaviness and uncertainty of their lives and find what they are missing. Here, they can enact old, suppressed emotions by crying and laughing with their heroes, thereby releasing them from their system in a safe setting because it's only a fantasy world. Used as such, it is a beautiful gift through which the empath can access and free suppressed emotions. However, this habit can also lead the empath to escape their life's problems whenever they seem too overwhelming to deal with. By distracting themselves from what needs attention, they are blocking positive changes in their life as a result.

For example, when the empath escapes an argument by crawling into one of his fantasy worlds to avoid having to feel what the argument has stirred up in him. The world of imagination then serves as a distraction until the wave of emotion has subsided, and that way, they can block out the incident. But by doing so, they fail to resolve the situation, and the circumstances will repeat themselves in the future.

Once you've brought light to your habit of mentally escaping, this shadow can become a wonderful way of creating more magic and awe in your life. While many people need intentional training to activate their imaginative skills, it comes naturally for you. So, don't be shy to use that gift, but do it as consciously as possible. Understand that there is nothing wrong with having an introverted side; if anything, the opposite is true. How cool is it to have a safe space in your mind?

It's great to have a strategy that helps you cope with situations where you feel overwhelmed. Just try to observe it as consciously as possible for you in that present moment, and reconnect to yourself as soon as you feel capable again.

I want to encourage you to keep dreaming but to do it consciously and purposefully. To make it your superpower, because then your ability to disappear into fantasy worlds can be seen as the beautiful gift that it was meant to be. I'm so happy that you get to experience these mind adventures, but at the same time, I want to advise you not to let your current life fall by the wayside. I promise you that if you start walking the path of self-knowledge and become aware of the magic within yourself and within this world, you can create your own real-life adventure.

I still love letting myself sink deep into a good book, movie, or daydream. But at the same time, I do it much less than I used to because my real life on this planet Earth has become my favorite and most heroic story. Realizing that will bring you an even deeper and, above all, lasting satisfaction. It will fulfill the deep longing within you so much more than a fantasy world ever could. You will feel that you have arrived in your own story as your own hero.

2. TENDENCY TO PEOPLE-PLEASE

The second typical shadow behavior I want to examine is people-pleasing. If you were raised by caretakers who were easily irritable and emotionally reactive, you might have developed the habit of trying to make other people happy when you're around them. When your well-being and the level of affection you received depended on pleasing your caretaker as much as possible, you've learned a subconscious program of "to experience peace and security in the presence of another person, I need to make sure that person is happy."

So many empaths learned early on to scan the room for whoever might not be pleased and then try to figure out how they could change that. And here, many even start prioritizing the well-being of those around them over their own. As soon as someone expresses their anger in their presence, they may immediately question whether there's the slightest possibility they might have caused the other person's distress instead of first acknowledging that they're now distressed as well and need support themselves. Comforting others becomes a way of comforting themselves.

They might be the first to notice tension in a conversation between others and feel the urgent need to step in and calm the situation before anyone explodes. This pattern can feel especially exhausting and create the impression that being around others and feeling comfortable requires hard work or that true rest is only possible while being alone. Once you've learned how to feel safe in your own presence, there is no need to constantly please others.

One of the biggest lessons for you as an empath lies in allowing yourself to please yourself first and learning that you are safe even if you don't constantly please everyone else around you. Learn how to stay present with yourself while there is uncomfortable energy in the room. Learn to give up the responsibility of handling difficult emotions for others and understand that they have nothing to do with you. Instead, turn to yourself in an act of self-love and prioritize your own need for comfort in the situation.

When the empath learns how to stay present and grounded in themselves and their own truth, they finally can allow themselves to be fully authentic in the company of others. Then, the ability to understand other people's needs and the desire to help becomes a beautiful gift instead of a heavy burden. Suddenly, they start coming from a place of consciously choosing to make others feel good instead of feeling one has to please them to maintain peace.

Then, this shadow aspect can turn into the beautiful gift of spreading good energy, sensing the needs of others, and understanding what it might take to defuse a tense situation. Not because you feel responsible to do so but because you want to spread your own inner peace. The empath can, for example, easily use these skills to help an insecure person feel safer in a situation.

3. TROUBLE SETTING BOUNDARIES

Along with the habit of people-pleasing, we often find a lack of boundaries in empaths. Their boundaries usually weren't respected as a child. A parent might have violated their right to have their own opinion or forced their expectations onto the child, teaching them to disregard their own boundaries in order to avoid rejection.

If you struggle with taking on the emotions of others, this shadow will help you understand why. One of the biggest blind spots empaths face is the suffering they experience out of empathy. When we're empathic, we resonate with someone else's vibrational state and adapt to it. We start vibrating at the same frequency they do. So we start feeling the same way. If there is no boundary between the experience of others and one's own experience, everybody's suffering becomes one's own—meaning that a lot of the suffering empaths face isn't even theirs.

This is the reason why so many empaths have a history of depression or emotional burnout. They are loaded with heavy emotions, which they pick up from the world around them, and turn numb to their own needs for recharge and self-care until they run out of energy. Then, they lose the resources they need to be able to fulfill their desire to help.

This boundless empathy often stems from the empath's childhood wound of feeling different—like an alien—not truly belonging and not being seen and understood. To cope with their chronic feelings of loneliness, they preferred to compromise their boundaries for the sake of others. This allowed them to feel connected to others and to experience a sense of closeness. As a child, this mechanism undoubtedly saved the empath from complete isolation, which can be devastating at that young age. However, as an adult, the empath must realize that this misguided love will never truly benefit anyone.

Another aspect of this shadow is that the empath might expect others to open their boundaries in return; they might feel entitled to extra treatment or rejected if those around them prioritize themselves when the empath often doesn't. This feeling might even further encourage the empath to neglect their boundaries and thereby avoid disappointing others, as they have felt the pain of rejection and don't want anyone else to feel the same way. A dangerous cycle begins.

The secret to breaking this cycle lies in realizing the difference between being hurt and feeling hurt. If we feel hurt by something, it's not because we've been hurt but because we've been triggered and reminded of a past hurt or trauma. And as we've learned, from a shamanic perspective, every triggering situation is an opportunity to release old pain and heal, and therefore, a gift on the soul level. When you start observing the difference within yourself, you'll automatically stop taking everything personally, especially other people's boundaries.

Another way in which the lack of boundaries manifests is when empaths take on the stories that others project onto them. For example, if you start worrying about or even doubting your own behavior after an encounter because you sensed the other person's reaction as judgment, disapproval, or withdrawal.

Whenever you find yourself in such a situation, remember that whatever others might project onto you is their story, not yours. And nobody can force their story onto you if you won't allow it. If you worry about something you did or said, a very powerful question to recenter yourself in your own truth is: "How would I have felt if I saw someone behaving like me?"

To create a clear boundary in a current situation, the affirmation "What's yours is yours, what's mine is mine" can also be very helpful. This enables you to clearly distinguish between your own truth and the emotions you have absorbed from another. That way, you can allow them to keep their emotions while focusing on your own truth.

If this shadow resonated with you, you want to learn how to notice your own needs, especially when they often don't match the needs of those around you. Next, you'll want to acknowledge where you've hurt yourself by stepping over your own boundaries and forgiving yourself for doing so. Suppressed resentment of yourself can be a serious blockage to self-love and seeing your self-worth. It's important to acknowledge yourself and that you are always doing your best with where you're at.

To fully heal this shadow, you have to get to the root of your separation pain. With practice, this shadow can turn into the beautiful gift of oneness consciousness. As someone who is fluid with boundaries and trained to tune into other people's perspectives and feelings, you can get a bigger picture of the collective consciousness. Now, you also have the ability to consciously open up to and adopt the vibrations that uplift and support you. You can even open up to certain abilities of others and allow them to grow within you as well, simply by sensing and absorbing the vibration behind those qualities.

EXERCISE: SPOT YOUR BOUNDARIES

Whenever you find yourself unclear of your boundaries, take a moment to focus on your body consciousness. Feel into your avatar and notice what it's like to be "your human name." Explore the physical boundaries of your being by lightly tapping over your body. Notice the emotional, mental, and spiritual boundaries of your being and listen to yourself.

You might ask yourself: am I feeling comfortable and safe? Or are my boundaries being compromised? Feel into yourself and see whether your body is tense or relaxed. When we are relaxed, this is often a good sign that our boundaries have been respected. A helpful question to challenge old thought patterns can also be: "If everything were allowed, where would my boundary be here?" or "If it were guaranteed that I would still be loved and acknowledged by everyone involved, where would my boundary be in this situation?"

EXERCISE: AFFIRMATIONS FOR HEALTHY BOUNDARIES

Affirmations are an excellent tool for training your subconscious mind and forming new habits. The following are examples of affirmations that may help you create new healthy habits around boundaries. To find the right fit for you, speak them out loud and see how each of them makes you feel.

"I am not responsible for the feelings of others!"

"I am allowed to have boundaries and to express them!"

"I am allowed to make others feel uncomfortable!"

"It is safe for me to be authentically myself!"

"I am me!"

"I own my space!"

"I don't like others too close in my space!"

"This is my boundary!"

You can pick the phrase that resonates most and practice it daily. Of course, you can also create your own mantra. Whatever you choose, speak it out loud at least three times in a row. Become more familiar with the phrase. Understand its meaning and build an intimate connection with it. Let it sink deep into your system.

You can also try to combine speaking your mantra with tapping on your body, helping your system integrate your intention even deeper and leave your body feeling powerful and confident. This can be very helpful in situations where you feel anxious and need to ground yourself back into your body and your truth. Experiment with the intensity and location of the tapping, and listen to how your body responds and what serves its needs best. This exercise might sound simple but can be super powerful if practiced sincerely.

EXERCISE: INNER CHILD CONTEMPLATION ON ANGER

Another thing that is very common for people who struggle with boundaries is suppressed anger. I've seen this with many empaths. If they feel any anger at all, it is often only subliminal and directed at themselves or shows in sudden, unpredictable outbursts of rage. They have probably experienced anger as something terrible that was not lived healthily and a threat to their well-being.

Many of us also tend to associate anger with guilt. That is, once the child shows their boundaries through anger, most parents can't deal with it healthily and blame the child for displaying the emotion. Guilt is one of the worst feelings a child can have, so as a consequence, they often learn to bury their anger indefinitely.

Of course, our goal is not to become destructively angry. In fact, outbursts of anger in empaths are usually a sign of how much they tend to repeatedly override their anger and boundaries until one day they explode. Healthy anger, on the other hand, is something that gives us clarity and strength. Clarity on where we fail to honor our boundaries and where our limits are being violated and strength to change that and help us stand up for ourselves. So precisely to strengthen your I-awareness, the emotion of anger is one of our strongest helpers, as it points out whenever our boundaries are crossed.

For this exercise, meet your inner child in meditation as instructed earlier. Visualize your young self, and start a conversation by asking why it doesn't want to feel anger. What past experiences have led to your current relationship with anger? Let them show you a situation that had to do with anger and was very hurtful for the little one. Step into this situation as an adult and protect your younger self. See how innocent this little child is and that it should have been worth more!

Allow your anger to speak, and tell the person involved in the situation at the time what needs to be said with powerful clarity. Stand between them and your inner child and be the adult you needed back then! Then, pick up your younger self and get it out of this situation completely. It is now safe with you, and you take care of it. Tell your inner child all the supportive words you needed to hear back then. Give all the love you were missing. And happily show your inner child your flame of anger, which will protect you from now on and may even grow over time and become more and more powerful.

4. WANTS TO BE THE SAVIOR FOR OTHERS

One of the empath's biggest weak spots lies in their savior complex: they want to free everyone around them from suffering. While empaths are known for their big, open heart and love of helping people, the empath's underlying need to free themselves is often overlooked. Empaths are easily overwhelmed by the flood of emotions and feelings constantly surrounding them. Especially when their external world mirrors back their inner suffering. So, one reason to save others is to avoid their own feelings of overwhelm.

As children, Empaths often felt like they had to save their parents as they were incapable of holding themselves. As a child, we naturally want to do everything in our power to help our parents. Their helplessness is unbearable for us as children because our parents are our safety net, so if they are unstable, there is no sense of security at all. The child then takes on a responsibility that is way too big to carry for them and takes this pattern into adulthood.

Also, as a child, being there for others often gave the empath a sense of being needed and, therefore, worthy of existing in a space. When the empath feels needed, it calms their anxiety about getting abandoned. If someone needs them, they won't want to leave. In this context, empaths oftentimes mistake feeling needed for feeling loved because many never received the love they truly longed for as a child, so they substituted it with the feeling of being needed and gained a sense of intimacy from that.

So the empath projects their inner wound of not being saved onto the people around them in the form of deep empathy for others' pain and the desire to comfort others' inner children instead of their own, hoping that this person will make them feel loved in return. Their learned strategy is that it's easier to care for others than to care for themselves and face one's own heavy emotions that they never learned to deal with.

Here lies another big danger of this shadow because this tendency leaves the empath vulnerable to drawing people into their lives who carry an inner child just as helpless and wounded as their own. Since they radiate this energy of being the savior, they resonate with people who seek to be saved. The problem here is that in most cases, the Empath doesn't have the capacity to care for them, as they are still searching to rescue themselves.

These relationships are often characterized by trying hard but it never being enough, and the empath quickly gets into a spiral of constantly devaluing and blaming themself because they can't live up to their own standards. At the same time, the other person is incapable of giving the empath the love they truly desire, so the relationship is marked by lots of pain and disappointment. The empath might want to help but fails to realize that they are dealing with people who cannot be helped by another. Just like the empath, they need to learn to save themselves.

Some empaths might even put themselves in the role of the savior out of a need to be "special" because they aren't feeling special the way they are. Self-love is a key to healing the old pain and transforming this shadow into the beautiful gift that lies underneath: the deep compassion to help others.

When the empath loves themselves first, they know how to fill their cup first and then give from a place of abundance instead of desperation. That is how the empath can bring light into their world and inspire others to truly heal themselves by becoming a role model.

5. ATTRACTS TOXIC RELATIONSHIPS

This shadow might be the most interesting one for empaths: their tragic attraction to toxic relationships, in which all of the previously discussed shadows come together. Since empaths often carry a deep subconscious longing for connection, they tend to idealize people a lot. They are visionaries and dreamers, so it's especially easy to inspire their hopes, which then turn into strong filters for anything the empath perceives. Their understanding nature makes it easy for them to see the good in people, and so they do.

It's almost as if they were wearing tainted glasses, which make everyone seem trustworthy. And out of their desperate longing for connection, they tend to project their own romantic feelings onto others, assuming they'd feel the same. Because of past childhood experiences, they often don't recognize red flags as many of them were accepted as normal to them their whole life. They might even block them from their consciousness as they might not know they deserve better. Another problem is the self-doubt empaths often naturally face and their fragile sense of self, which makes them vulnerable to gaslighting and manipulation.

When these shadows aren't integrated, the empath likely tends to attract someone with whom they share a trauma bond. That means someone who replays their trauma. The empath might attract a toxic relationship in which they—as described in Savior Shadow—resume responsibilities that are not theirs and try to save their partner, but in doing so, will never be enough. Or they attract a partner who treats them very poorly and, in this way, makes them feel as unloved and worthless as their childhood experiences. The cycle of trauma repeats itself.

Every reoccurring cycle is a possibility to self-realize, become aware of one's shadow habits and underlying pains, and heal them. The old wound is reopened, and the pain is so intense that one cannot look away. Not anymore. The path to healing, in most cases, then has to be walked alone.

This shadow is another invitation to strengthen your boundaries and center yourself in your frame. The more you learn to comfort yourself and hold your energy, the less you will crave that feeling from the external world. Don't try to suppress the feeling of longing, but rather investigate it. Listen to it and ask it questions, such as: "What is it that I am truly longing for?", "Is there pain underneath this longing that wants to be cried out?", "Is there any way I can meet the need behind this longing by myself?". Maybe you can set aside some dedicated time and have a date with yourself, knowing that only by caring for the relationship with yourself can and will you learn to attract people who care for you on that same level and beyond. You have to choose yourself first.

You are worthy of realizing how magical, powerful, lovable, adorable, and special you are to this world, regardless of what you do. If you notice this shadow, you can hug it lovingly and admit your doubts about yourself. You can feel and love this shadow and tell yourself how valuable you are!

The hidden gift in this shadow is your innate ability to see the good in people, which is a beautiful trait empaths have. Being able to see the light in others and look at their potential can be one of your greatest strengths if you don't blend out the shadow aspects while doing so.

Seeing not only the light but also the shadow in those around you will help you figure out who will positively influence your life and who will likely drain your energy. Seeing clearly will enable you to make wise relationship decisions and help you understand that unconditional love doesn't mean unconditional tolerance!

To fully heal this shadow, you have to get to the root of your lack of self-worth. You need to understand your own story and pain, find deep compassion for yourself, and, out of this love for yourself, create a new growing self-worth.

Remember that the deep connection you're craving, and the only connection that can ever give you the full sense of oneness, is the connection to yourself, your soul, and the great oversoul. To cultivate this connection, you can work on connecting to your higher self and your inner child through meditation, dance, prayer, chanting, or journaling. Spend time with your soul, and let your soul spend time with your human. Visualize the great oversoul all around you, giving you all the love you ever craved for. Soon, you will realize that oneness is achieved internally first.

Your shadow is a powerful invitation to become one with yourself again. Fully empowered. So, let's figure out how to draw out your story and the hidden gifts in your shadow.

HOW TO TURN YOUR SHADOWS INTO GIFTS

When we discover our shadows for the first time, we often see them as problems which couldn't be further from the truth. In reality, they were the much-needed solution at a specific time in your life! Your system was trying to protect you from something that was too painful. It found strategies to help you survive in this world and your childhood home. The shadow was the solution to a much deeper problem. The fact that this world here wasn't a safe place for you but a threat to your well-being.

When we become aware of our shadows, we tend to judge them as somehow faulty when they are actually old declarations of love from ourselves to ourselves—the attempt to enable us to deal with this world. To see them as that and to meet them lovingly changes everything. That is why it is so important not only to recognize the superficial shadow but also to recognize the trauma that underlies it. There, we find deep understanding for ourselves and thereby allow healing to flow into our being.

Over time, your shadows will dissolve more and more because they are no longer needed. If you meet a shadow, ask yourself: What else do I need it for? Where do I not yet feel completely safe? Not quite loved yet? Not always enough? To what extent does this shadow behavior serve me? And give your system time to unlearn this shadow behavior. They have served you for so many years, and, of course, they have also strengthened as a structure. Now, they are allowed to gently loosen again until, one day, you are amazed to find that they no longer play out.

Be loving with yourself and your system. Grateful for what the shadows gave you. These frequencies of love and gratitude are very high and will bring miracles into your life and a sense of deep peace. You don't need to fight your shadow behaviors; you may turn them into love.

The following exercise will help you learn how to build and maintain healthy relationships with yourself and others and present you with a deeper understanding of your own system.

EXERCISE: FINDING YOUR HIDDEN STORIES

Whenever you find yourself getting triggered by a situation, unable to understand why you react in such an intense way, use the following questions to trace your shadow. They will help you to integrate them into everyday situations and to activate their underlying gifts. These questions are structured in a sensible order. However, always follow your intuition if you feel guided to answer them in an alternative order.

1. The trigger: What situation triggered your emotional reaction?

2. The thoughts: What thoughts does this situation trigger in you? Do you recognize a familiar voice in them?

3. The emotions: What emotions and sensations does this situation trigger in you? - Try to immerse yourself in this emotion for a few minutes but only to that extent, which allows you to remain present and grounded at the same time.

4. Remember the trauma behind the shadow: Where do you know this feeling from? Maybe your childhood?

5. Deep conviction: What deep basic convictions and beliefs emerged at that time?

6. New beliefs: What new, healing beliefs can you find for your inner child? What would you have needed back then? – Imagine how you hold your former self in your arms, give them a lot of love, and explain to them that you can now live according to the new belief.

7. Open up to a bigger picture: After feeling through your old emotions, open yourself to new worldviews and look again at the situation with curiosity and open eyes. What other truths might exist about this situation?

8. Shadow behavior: Which shadow behavior can you detect?

9. The gift: What gifts can you discover in your shadow? Are there specific strengths you can develop by working through this situation?

10. Growth: What can you do to reap these gifts?

11. The here and now: What feelings and thoughts do you have now about the situation? Is there anything that you can feel gratitude for?

To give you a deeper understanding of these questions and make it easier to work with them in the future, I've created example answers for you:

1. The trigger: What situation triggered your emotional reaction?

I want to hang out with my friends, but when I call them and ask, they are busy, so I end up alone and feeling rejected.

2. The thoughts: What thoughts does this situation trigger in you? Do you recognize a familiar voice in them?

"Nobody wants me." "I'll never ask again." "This person doesn't appreciate me as a friend." Maybe my mother's voice? Did she feel the same?

3. The emotions: What emotions and sensations does this situation trigger in you? - Try to immerse yourself in them for a few minutes but only to that extent, which allows you to remain present and grounded at the same time.

I feel a tightness in my chest, heaviness in my heart, an uncomfortable burning sensation in my stomach, and my jaw is clenched. I detect sorrow, grief, humiliation, loneliness, desperation, anger.

4. Remember the trauma behind the shadow: Where do you know this feeling from? Maybe your childhood?

I remember how my mom used to withdraw and lock herself up in her bedroom whenever she wasn't feeling good or had a fight with my dad. I would get scared because there were so many hurt feelings, and I wanted comfort and reassurance from my mom, but she wouldn't talk to me and just disappeared. My dad would have this angry attitude and wasn't approachable, so I was left feeling alone and abandoned without understanding what I could've done to change it.

5. Deep conviction: What deep basic convictions and beliefs emerged at that time?

I am all alone in this world. Anyone who comes close might, sooner or later and at any given point in time, turn on me and leave me alone in my pain. I have to learn how not to need anyone and be fine with being alone. They might reject me if I need them to be around.

6. New beliefs: What new, healing beliefs can you find for your inner child? What would you have needed back then? – Imagine how you hold your former self in your arms, give them a lot of love, and explain to them that you can now live according to the new belief.

I will never reject myself! I am always here for myself, and that is enough. I can never be truly alone because I'm always with myself now. I don't need the company of someone else to feel complete. Other people's pain might disable them from feeling or showing love to me sometimes, but their love will always return and is never lost, even when it feels like that sometimes. It is safe to be rejected; it has nothing to do with my value or the love of my counterpart for me. And if that happens, I am there for myself!

7. Open up to a bigger picture: After feeling through your old emotions, open yourself to new worldviews and look again at the situation with curiosity and open eyes. What other truths might there be about this situation?

My friend might need some alone space to practice self-care and, therefore, be the friend they can be. I can be a good friend by giving them the room they need and being there once they feel like hanging out again. The fact that they don't have time for me right now has nothing to do with me personally or the fact that they don't want me anymore. My friends love me even if they are busy.

8. Shadow behavior: Which shadow behavior can you detect?

I have a habit of withdrawing from people without hearing them out. I want to avoid the feeling of getting rejected, and therefore, automatically assume that I am unwanted and remove myself without looking at the situation objectively.

9. The gift: What gifts can you discover in your shadow? Are there specific strengths you can develop by working through this situation?

My shadow behavior is a form of love for myself. I withdraw so quickly because I want to protect myself from being rejected and having to feel the old pain. So, in this shadow lies the gift of taking good care of myself and having a deep understanding of myself. The situation gives me the gift of getting to my old pain and feeling it through. So, this old wound may become visible, and my emotional charge may flow off. In this, I can find even more love and understanding for myself and strengthen the relationship between myself and my inner child.

10. Growth: What can you do to reap this gift?

Whenever I feel rejected, instead of withdrawing, I can talk to my friends, let them know how I am feeling, and then hear them out. They might tell me they are just tired and would love to see me some other time. When I understand their perspective, I can let go of the overthinking stories of my past trauma and, when it shows, feel through my old pain. I can take time to hug my inner child and explain that we don't have to take it personally. We can just do something fun and hang out with our friends some other time.

11. The here and now: What feelings and thoughts do you have now about the situation? Is there anything for which you can feel gratitude?

Once I allow the situation to be what it is and accept it, I open myself up to finding ways to spend quality time with just me. I feel gratitude for the universe for arranging the circumstances so I have time to learn this. And when I am content and deeply connected to myself, I feel much better about being with my friend and our encounter can take on a new quality that is not built on dependency.

PSYCHIC PERCEPTION

*N*ow that we've understood the empathic gift and learned how to integrate our shadows as strengths, we are ready to take a closer look at the psychic aspect of the empathic ability. So, what does it mean to be or become psychic?

THE METAPHYSICS OF PSYCHIC ABILITIES

The word psyche is of ancient Greek origin and is translated as soul or spirit. It refers to the life energy that inhabits our body yet doesn't seem to be material. In psychology, it's used to describe the totality of our mind, both conscious and unconscious. It's the spirit, the immaterial part of our being.

Psychic abilities are, therefore, any skills of using only your mental and spiritual energy to read or influence the world around you as opposed to through the body, which we as humans are used to navigating our material world with. For the most part, we are focused on our five physical senses to interact with our surroundings. But what if our world is much deeper and more complex than our five physical senses can perceive?

For a long time, scientists assumed that our physical reality was the primary phenomenon, but modern-day metaphysics discovered that matter, which makes up our physical world, behaves like waves on a subatomic level. Everything we perceive as solid is made up of energy that moves in such a way and frequency that it creates the illusion of a solid mass.

This illusion of matter is created by our five senses, which pick up a certain frequency and translate it into a specific impression, such as an image or a sound. So when you look at the human body-mind-complex as a machine to navigate the world we live in and make it "readable," our five senses are the basic program you need to navigate this realm. But they can only reveal the physical manifestation of any phenomenon.

Psychic abilities or clair senses are the upgrades to those programs. They enhance your ability to perceive reality on an energetic level to the point that you are suddenly able to decode beyond the physical realm into the realms of energy. This can be hearing or feeling the thoughts of others, seeing their energy field or aura, or suddenly knowing the next sequence of events before they actually happen.

In many ancient cultures and throughout history, shamans have been the masters and teachers of these psychic abilities. The word shaman originated from the Tungus tribe in Siberia and translated to "the one who sees in the dark." Shamans traditionally have always been the ones who saw where most humans are blind—in the energy realm. They have been described as those who lived in both worlds at the same time, the physical and the so-called world of the spirits, the energy, or the astral realms.

These realms are non-physical realities that run parallel to our own reality, some of which we all enter at night while sleeping. But also in daydreams, where we create the blueprint of what can manifest in our physical world. Shamans are the ones who perceive energy before it becomes physical, and therefore, throughout time, they have been sought out by humans to assist in the healing of the mind, body, and spirit.

As an empath, you feel beyond the limitations of your body and physical senses. By tuning into someone else's energy, you perceive with your psyche. Empathy in its refined and mastered stages is indeed a form of clairsentience that enables you to experience subtle energy in the form of emotions of others by feeling them yourself. Therefore, your perception exceeds the average human range, which is confined to one's emotions and sentiments. You are already psychic.

If we see our senses as energy sensors that can perceive certain frequency ranges, we can see how our perception changes as we fine-tune these sensors to a higher sensitivity. This might feel like everything becomes louder, but you might also be able to perceive things you once didn't know existed. All five senses can become psychic abilities as they get more and more fine-tuned, and every human can fine-tune their senses with intention and consistency. The most common to find in people are clairvoyance (clear sight), clairaudience (clear hearing), claircognizance (intuitive knowing), and clairsentience (clear feeling). When trained properly, these senses are your most powerful tool for energy work.

THE PSYCHIC SENSES AND THE CHAKRAS

While our physical senses are needed for us to navigate the physical world, our psychic senses help us navigate the energy realms, which create the blueprint for our physical reality. Our psychic senses are also our connection to wisdom, or what shamanism refers to as the energy of Father Sky, the all-knowing aspects of our divine soul.

They are our connection to divine masculine or yang energy. Metaphorically speaking, they are our connection to the upper world. Every psychic sense connects to a specific chakra. The word chakra is Sanskrit and translates to wheel or circle. It is used to refer to the seven main energy centers in which all of the energy channels of both our physical and subtle bodies flow together and charge. They are located along our spine, with the upper three making the throat and head area. They are namely:

— The crown chakra, which connects us to universal consciousness and our intuition through the sense of clear knowing or claircognizance.

— The brow chakra or third eye, which connects us to our divine vision and creative insights through the sense of clear vision or clairvoyance.

— And the throat chakra, which connects us to divine sound through the sense of clear hearing or clairaudience.

All these three energy centers are direct doorways into perceiving and communicating to our own superconscious, the part of us that exists beyond time and space and has, therefore, an omnipotent overview of all our life circumstances. Through these energy centers, we can perceive guidance from all higher intelligence and entities that exist beyond our earthly physical realms. These can be deceased loved ones, spirit guides, ancestors, or angels that can support us in our healing work and that we can call upon in ritual or meditation.

Through our yang chakras, we have access to our highest ideals, most genius epiphanies, and most inspired future visions. We see beyond what is and get an overview of the bigger picture of reality, beyond time and space, and beyond what we find in our present moment. To access the full powers and gifts that your psychic abilities bring, your lower and higher chakras need to be balanced. The lower energy centers are our connection to life force and vitality or—from a shamanic perspective—they are our connection to Mother Earth, the all-nurturing life force, and the creative aspects of our divine soul. They are our connection to divine feminine or yin energy.

Metaphorically speaking, they are our connection to the lower world, the seat of our subconscious animal-like nature. They are namely:

— The root chakra, which connects us to our sense of security through the ability to ground the highest principles in the physical world and infuse them into the present moment.

— The sacral chakra connects us to our creational power through the ability to use our life force energy to manifest.

— And the solar plexus chakra, the connection to our human story and our ability to transform it.

These chakras connect our soul to the physical world, through which we create the ideas we've perceived from the higher realms and through our psychic abilities. Through our yin chakras, we have access to our deepest desires, most motivating emotions, and most hidden secret fears and roadblocks, but also to our power to create and transform.

When we start opening up our upper chakras to the infinite wisdom, inspiration, and insights of the universe, we will increasingly experience energy downloads into our being. And since things in our universe have to always be in flow by nature, this energy has to go somewhere. It has to be grounded in the Earth, or it will overwhelm our system.

To step into our full potential as human beings, and especially as psychic empaths, we need our yin and yang energies balanced. This balance is secured and reinforced by our middle energy center, the heart chakra, or the seat of our present consciousness. The heart center is what anchors us in the moment and connects us to the quantum field of unconditional love and acceptance, which turns your empathic ability psychic. Then, you'll experience the full spectrum of your clairsentience by staying deeply connected to what is, both in the physical and energetical realm. The heart center is where both the yang and yin energies meet, fall in love, dance together, reinforce each other, and then burst back with greater power. Love connects these two energies and attracts them toward each other to mix and create worlds.

So, when opening up the higher chakras to work with your psychic senses, you want to ensure that you are well-grounded in your lower chakras and well-centered in your heart space at all times.

One big reason I put so much emphasis on shadow work in this book is that if we only look at the superconscious and psychic abilities but have not integrated our subconscious well, our energy work will suffer. If I only work with the superconscious, my shadows will play out unconsciously. I am no longer connected to Earth. We see this, for example, in some people who follow the spiritual path and are suddenly no longer accessible to human feelings. They seem to be above everything, but de facto, can no longer get involved in relationships.

These people tend to talk a lot about concepts and philosophies but exclude essential aspects of being human. They often do what is referred to as spiritual bypassing, where they focus on all the blissful parts of spiritual living and create huge blind spots around anything that feels negative or doesn't fit their ideal of the highest perspective on life. This can even show up as fleeing into the higher realms as an escape from earthly existence, as I did in my previous life.

Wholesome spiritual living means taking the highest perspective, the highest light, and shining it onto the darkest part of your being and reality, not ignoring the pain but sending love and wisdom into it to heal. In the same way, if we focus only on the subconscious, we won't ever access our highest potential.

A person who only deals with their subconscious could get lost in the so-called "healing cycle" (even though the term "fixing cycle" would be much more accurate). They still want to heal this and that and forget their own divine nature and that they were always whole. They bog down in the depths and thus do not manifest any great visions in their life. Instead, they get trapped in an endless chase for their shadows, which are infinite.

Practically, the subconscious is accessed through work with the inner child and shadow work, while the superconscious is accessed through work with the soul and your connection to the universe.

THE IMPORTANCE OF HEART-CENTERED WORK

In the middle of the yang and the yin chakras, we'll find the heart chakra, in which both energies meet to form a powerful union that creates an electro-magnetic field around us. This field is our ultimate source of love. It enables us to connect to the greater all on a very physical and grounded level. If we are tuned into our heart center, we act from a felt experience of oneness, which creates compassion towards our surroundings and selflessness, the foundation for true service. To ensure your actions and messages are supported by divine love and in alignment with the highest good of all, you should make sure to always tune into your heart field before tapping into your psychic abilities.

By grounding yourself in your heart space, you graduate your ability to feel empathy for others to feeling compassion. Thereby, you move into the full power of your clairsentience, which will also enable you to keep your balance and let any emotions flow through your system without losing yourself in them. That is because compassion connects you to the awareness of everything that is. Or what shamans see as the one big soul consciousness we all share and have access to on a deeper level. This connection will add a subtle feeling of peace and acceptance to any situation.

While empathy is the fully felt experience of a connection with another, the higher levels of consciousness and the boundaries to hold that high level are often missing. Empathy is not rooted in source frequency, whereas compassion is deeply grounded. By tapping into your heart energy, you connect the truth of the lower world with the higher realms of the upper world—you transform empathy into compassion. In this way, you tune into the highest perspective in every situation, connecting to the divine soul's endless wisdom and unconditional love while simultaneously experiencing the raw truth of emotions.

Now, you will be able to see both the vulnerability of being a human and the true greatness of the soul. Now, you will be able to approach both your own and someone else's suffering in loving kindness instead of drowning in the pain. Now, you will naturally say the right things to make others feel seen, understood, and supported because you are actually feeling with them while at the same time being firmly grounded in the healing energies of universal love.

Being heart-centered will also prevent you from projecting any of your shadow stories onto others, which we all do to an extent. If you, for example, carry the trauma of neglect, you might feel especially sorry for people who remind you of your own past and wounds, even those who are happy with their own ways. You might think that if certain energies trigger horrible feelings in you, it must, therefore, feel just as bad for others when that isn't necessarily the case. Acting from a heart-centered place of love allows you to tune into the other one's best interest and listen to what they want and need with your whole being, opening yourself up to all possibilities.

In the end, your enormous capacity to empathize with any person or situation is such a beautiful enhancement of life. Once it's transformed into compassion, it automatically stops causing you pain and suffering. Then it's not your weak spot anymore but the foundation for all the healing work you can do in the world. Then, you are one of the few individuals who have mastered true compassion. Then, you have fully unleashed your empathic superpower. A power that is desperately needed in our modern-day world!

So whenever you are working with energy, there are a few fundamental practices that are the basis and should, therefore, be cultivated with intention and care to give you the best ground to stand on. These practices are centering, grounding, and holding space. The following practices will provide you with this solid foundation, and their effects will develop in potency when trained consistently over time. The more you master these basic tools and integrate them into your psychic practice, the stronger your powers can manifest.

1. CENTERING

The first important basic practice is centering oneself. That's because, as discussed, centering yourself before you engage in energy work will ensure that you're acting from a place of balance and harmony—free from subconscious projections. Tuning into your heart field will connect you to the core vibration of the universe, as we described earlier, which is loving oneness, and therefore aligns all your perspectives, actions, and thoughts with the highest possible frequency of unconditional love.

If you can listen with your heart, you will experience a sense of communion with the divine and all that exists. Here, you will tap into what witches describe as perfect love and perfect trust, a state of bliss and mild euphoria that will make you feel like you've been activated to live life in a new way. When you are centered, you are empowered and confident. This practice will reveal to you the divine soul in those around you and enable you to surrender yourself to the well-being of all. It also allows you to be fully present with what anchors you in the current moment, open and receptive.

EXERCISE: CENTERING MEDITATION

Take your preferred meditation position and close your eyes. Bring your awareness to yourself as the center of your reality. Acknowledge that everything in your perception happens around you. You are the vortex of your universe.

Now zoom out of that perspective. See yourself getting smaller and smaller. Zoom further out, overseeing your house, the area around you, your city, country, and planet Earth. With every zoom-out, you open up your field wider and wider to a higher consciousness. Zoom out further and further into the solar system and the galaxy until you reach the very edge of your universe. Here, you find a crystal holding everything. Watch how this crystal sends beams of unconditional love and wisdom from the edge of the universe right into your heart center. Feel how your heart recharges that divine source of energy. Stay here for as long as you wish, and then zoom back down to your human perspective right into your heart space. You are centered.

2. GROUNDING

Grounding your energy will be the next important step in your energy work routine. I would like to explain the importance of grounding with the example of an electrical charge. The first thing one learns when dealing with huge amounts of electricity is the need to ground and discharge any excess energy into Earth, where it is then neutralized. Without proper grounding, the energy would hit the subject in full force, fry it, and leave permanent damage.

And what goes for electrical energy also applies to all other forms of energy. If we are exposed to intense or heavy energies, they often become too much, can overwhelm our system, and lead to psychic burnout. This is why grounding should be a habitual practice you perform before and after every healing session you engage in. Not only that, especially in situations when you feel a sensory overload or are being hit with an especially unpleasant and heavy emotion, you can use grounding to relieve yourself and pass it onto Earth.

At the same time, grounding is not only the best way to release unwanted energy but also an infinite source of high-frequency energy to recharge and nurture yourself. Earth is, after all, our big cosmic mother, who holds unconditional love, support, and healing for us. Grounding is your most important way of staying connected to that source of wisdom and power. To give you a few examples of how diverse grounding can look like:

It can be a walk in nature, a drum circle, a barefoot walk, gardening, feeling the ground, a meeting with your inner child, painting or drawing, journaling, practicing gratitude, connecting with others, moving your body, massaging yourself, taking a bath, talking to a friend, cooking and eating, especially root vegetables and legumes (e.g. potatoes, carrots, lentils, chickpeas, etc.) or anything that connects you to Earth, your body and being human. Regular quality sleep is also very important for the body and psyche to be properly grounded.

You can also try the following breathing exercise for grounding and relaxing your nervous system: breathe deeply, slowly, and evenly, and do it to the count of inhale 4—hold 7—exhale 8. Follow this rhythm until you feel calm and connected.

Another tip when you need immediate grounding is to name five things you see, hear, smell, and feel in your surroundings. You may name them out loud or quietly in your mind, but try to use full sentences, such as I see a green wall, feel soft sheets under my body, and hear the wind blow in the streets. This will help you stay grounded in your everyday life.

Whenever you engage your psychic abilities, you should make it a habit to ground yourself before and after, especially if you are working with other people. For that, you can use the following grounding meditation.

EXERCISE: GROUNDING MEDITATION

Find a comfortable position, either standing, sitting, or lying down. Close your eyes and start listening to your breathing. Now, bring your awareness to your root center, the point where your body touches the ground when you're sitting on the floor. Your lowest energy center is your connection to Earth. Imagine it like a red energy ball that slowly spins in your pelvic area.

Now, envision this ball releasing an energy cord down toward the ground underneath you. Use your willpower to extend the cord deeper into the ground with every exhale you take. See it pass through the floor of your building, through concrete, and deep into the Earth. See it reach deeper and deeper through layers of rock, underground caves, and streams of water until it reaches the vibrant, powerful magma core of the Earth. Envision Earth's core as this big red energy ball that spins in the same way your root center does. Hear it pulsate like a beating heart. Now, feel the connection between your root center and Earth's core. Feel her warm, loving energy rise up the cord and fill your being with strength and comfort. What's it like to be connected to Earth through a grounding cord?

Feel how all heavy and intense emotions and energies are released and passed down the cord to Mother Earth. Pass down whatever emotion or thought is too much to hold. She will gladly take it for you and transform it in her fire. Once you are done, tell her how grateful you are that she is holding space and relieving you from all those heavy burdens. Pull the energy cord back up to close the grounding session. Affirm to yourself: I am grounded.

Note: Find a beautiful recorded version of the grounding and centering meditation in our free meditation bundle.

3. HOLDING SPACE

The last basic practice I encourage you to make a habit of is connecting to the space around you before you start any energy work. The space surrounding you is your greatest ally in any ritual you perform. Shamanic traditions have taught us that everything is conscious, meaning it carries awareness of the great oversoul, including the space surrounding you at any time. Not only that, but it also responds to our energy field the same way all of existence does because the consciousness that inhabits the space around us is the same consciousness that our soul spark is made of at its deepest level.

Accessing and communing with this all-present, all-knowing consciousness has always been an essential ritual component for shamans. They knew that by honoring the space and asking it for support, they could create a powerful energy bubble around them and infuse the room with more healing energy. Through listening with all your senses, physical and psychic, you will know how to create the right environment for healing to take place.

This practice will help you connect to your energy allies and spirit guides. This is beneficial, especially if you want to practice healing work on others, as this will help you mobilize all available support. You will learn to offer the space for people to express their bottled-up emotions, explore their deep pains, mourn their losses, and give them company in facing their demons.

You will also learn how to provide comfort for them to let go and invoke an energy field in which they can meet their soul, thus bringing lasting transformation and healing. As an empath, you have the gift to accompany and guide through deep emotions with full compassion. Holding space allows you to release those energies right away, as they don't have to be held by you alone. Instead, they are held by existence and, therefore, in love. And love heals them all.

EXERCISE: OPENING AND CLOSING SPACE

When holding space, you'll always want to start by grounding and centering yourself. Use the grounding meditation to release all heavy emotions that might block or distract you and draw up the unconditional love of Earth. Zoom out of your own perspectives to get open for greater wisdom. Then, center the unconditional love together with the great universal wisdom in your heart space and anchor it there.

Now, with your eyes still closed, feel into the space around you. Notice how your breathing connects you to the outside world and how your breathing infuses your surroundings with your energy. Send your love into the space and feel how it changes the atmosphere. Now, picture the space around you as a conscious, living being; feel how it, too, breathes in and out, and notice how the space infuses your being with its energy. Now, thank the space around you for its support. Notice how existence always holds you in a loving embrace.

If you feel like calling in extra support to your ritual, you can use this moment to call in any spirit guides, like your guardian animal. Maybe you've set up an altar for your spirit allies and want to light a candle for them. This will greatly enhance your ritual space and help center the energies in the room. To deepen this practice, you may bring offerings to your altar, such as food and incense, or invoke the spirits of your affection by singing a mantra for them.

Once you are done with your session, you can close the healing space by again thanking the room as well as the spirits who participated for their support and willfully drawing your energy back into your center.

FOUR WAYS TO BUILD YOUR PSYCHIC SENSES

The fine-tuning of your senses to become super detectors is easier than you think. Because your psychic senses are like muscles that just need to be trained regularly, the more you use them, the more useful they will get, and the more you will notice them. So, for example, the psychic ability that likely comes easiest to you as an empath —feeling— can be refined by consciously observing what emotions and thoughts you perceive from your environment and distinguishing them from your own. The better you become at this, the more your confidence will naturally grow, and the more you will manifest your true power. Here, we will discuss some useful techniques and habits to develop and train your psychic senses.

1. MEDITATION

Meditation is your first and most important tool in learning to read and work with energy. There are many different ways in which meditation will help you expand your psychic abilities. While the meditations we discussed in previous chapters have focused mostly on working through emotions and shadows, this part is about training your focus and perception skills. And we will discuss different ways to achieve this goal. Meditation is one of the most common strategies because it is simple and comes with various side benefits. You will notice that once you start observing your mind, your perspective will expand, revealing a broader view of the picture.

By sitting and letting your mind calm down, you become still enough to perceive what's been hidden before—the deeper, energetic layers of existence. Because they've never really been hidden from you, you just weren't tuned into them fully, most likely distracted by your own thoughts. This is what meditation traditions point toward—we miss out on what is right in front of us because of our addiction to our own thought stream. Meditation trains you to zap out of that thought stream into the present moment, which always holds all the answers we ever need. When it comes to developing and strengthening your psychic skills, meditation is your power tool because to read energy, you need to become aware of it first.

For most humans nowadays, that means expanding our perception to pick up a more extensive range of different information. Our perception is constantly bombarded with millions of different impressions. They are all energetic information about our environment, such as the temperature, the different sounds, smells, and the subtle energetic bodies of people and things around us.

At any given point in our experience as human beings on Earth, there is an endless amount of information our system could pick up on. But as we only have a limited capacity to process all the impressions we take in, our brain filters out all information that does not appear important in the respective situation—in the same way, our brain learns to blend out our noses from our conscious sight. It's still there, and we can notice it if we focus our attention on our nose. But usually, we don't need to, and therefore, our sight perception pushes it into the background. So, if we want to learn to open up our conscious perception to pick up subtle energy, we need to train our awareness, and this is what meditation will commonly do.

Another significant aspect of meditation is how it lets us enter into what science calls the alpha brain wave state, the only state in which our subconscious and conscious are both accessible and directly interacting. It's commonly experienced right before falling asleep or right after waking up in the morning when dreams feel super vivid and intertwine with our real-life consciousness.

The brain state we access in meditation allows us to get into a state of deep relaxation, where we can commune, interact with universal consciousness, and receive energetic downloads. Often, these downloads are already present in your field, ready to inspire you or the answer to a long-asked question, and all they need to reach you is for you to relax and create space in your mind to receive them. To enhance your meditation experience, breathing techniques are powerful because they induce expanded states of consciousness and help distance us from our noisy thoughts.

EXERCISE: BASIC MEDITATION AND BREATHING EXERCISE

One of my favorite meditation practices to train basic meditative focus and concentration is connected breathing. To do this, find a quiet spot where you won't be disturbed. Generally, it's easiest to find calm and focus in the early morning or right before bed when the body naturally is ready to relax. Get into a comfortable position with your back straight and focus on your breathing. With every exhale, imagine letting go of the everyday impressions and creating space in your consciousness for the subtler pieces of information. Try to breathe gently but deeply without pausing at the end of each inhale and exhale. Just let them melt into each other as naturally as possible, like the ebb and flow of the ocean.

Notice how every inhale creates momentum for the exhale and vice versa. Imagine how, with each inhalation, the light energy around you breathes into you and connects you to everything that is while you simply relax. With each exhalation, you are breathing into the infinite room of existence. Feel your connection to everything through your breath, and become one with the field of wisdom and love that surrounds you at any time. Then, gently bring your attention back to the waves of your breathing and the stream of light flowing through you. Stay here for as long as you like. After a period of time, you can optionally ask for specific insights or have your awareness focus on specific pieces of information you wish to receive. Are there subtle energies and information in the room that you weren't aware of before? Or information that you picked up during the day but didn't have the capacity to consciously perceive? Let flow to you what wants to be received.

2. TRANCE

The next powerful way to tap into psychic information is through trance practices. In shamanic cultures, these date back to ancient traditions and, as such, have been practiced for thousands of years since the dawn of time. Trance is regarded as one of the most potent methods to bring forth the depths of the subconscious and superconscious, leading to profound transformation. That's because, in trance, we can easily slip into deeper states of consciousness, where our brain runs on theta and even delta waves. During these states, we not only get access to our subconscious as we do during meditative alpha states but fully emerge ourselves in them to the point of completely disconnecting from our waking awareness.

Throughout the ages, shamans danced—and still dance—in wild ecstasy, unleashing their abilities to perform healing and purification rituals. These shamans were aware of the exponentially stronger magic they could wield when their subconscious and superconscious minds conducted the rituals. They recognized the limitations of everyday consciousness and overcame them by slipping into transcendental mental spaces.

To enter these altered states, wild dances and drum journeys were employed, often accompanied by the enactment of specific formations and figures, ancient chants, or, at times, the utilization of psychedelic plants. Often, it was a fusion of numerous elements, blending together harmoniously. However, even in our present time, new paths have emerged to unlock these states. For instance, profound and prolonged breath sessions, such as the practice of holotropic breathing, have become avenues to open these mystical states for ourselves.

The trance experiences during these practices feel much like being under hypnosis, where you are in a mystical state of consciousness. They allow you to connect with your intuition, process trauma, and access spiritual guidance in a truly transformative way. In my own personal experience, the most profound and vivid visions and downloads have come to me through these trance rituals.

Every time you perform a ritual, you enter into your subconscious and superconscious mind, which brings you messages and reflects back to you where you are in your journey. Sometimes, it will bring forth images, symbols, or geometric patterns whose meaning your conscious self may not fully grasp but can sense intuitively.

If this occurs, you can follow up and further integrate your trance experience by reconnecting to the specific symbol or image and feeling into yourself, whether it came with the energy of wanting to be released or if it desires to come closer to you and to be embodied by you. You can work with your symbol by drawing it, possibly burning it afterward, or creating an altar infused with the energy from the trance. You can also lay a mandala in nature that resembles your symbol or express the trance experience through dance or chant.

Your subconscious understands symbols, images, and sounds on a much deeper level than words—therefore, it comprehends rituals that your conscious self can scarcely explain. And it transforms through these rituals far more rapidly than when we attempt to exert influence on our subconscious with our conscious selves. Even though the mind might not always understand, your heart, soul, and especially your body will. In essence, while performing rituals, we are speaking the language of the subconscious directly.

Through trance rituals, you connect with the spiritual realm and gain access to your inner wisdom. These practices allow you to tap into your innate psychic abilities and strengthen your bond with the divine. Furthermore, trance states are particularly useful for those who have gone through trauma and require access to their inner resources to heal. This is because they allow us to access deeply hidden emotions and release them on a very physical level as well. Oftentimes, through involuntary movements, which are ways the body releases energy blockages and old trauma, creating space for new energy.

When practiced correctly, the discussed practices can lead to lasting personal growth and transformation. At the same time, ecstatic trance is undoubtedly a state that can be quite stressful for the body, in contrast to traditional meditation. When combined with deep release and relaxation, however, this tension that arises has the potential to release a lot of old information and energy blockages from the body.

Trance is definitely one of the more intense ways to enter other levels of consciousness. They can induce profound and sometimes bewildering experiences where we no longer have the security of our conscious selves. It is possible to enter very extreme states, such as reliving an old, still-lingering trauma, reliving a past life, or even leaving one's own body. This means that a deep inner sense of security is necessary to process certain experiences wholesomely on your own. So always make sure to be firmly grounded before engaging in any trance practices so that you can truly derive healing from them and not become overwhelmed by this high energy. Keep in mind that faster is not always better, and we should generally approach trance practices with respect.

With that being said, there are gentler ways to enter a trance state, as well as more intense methods (such as holotropic breathing or plant medicine). For beginners, I recommend the latter only with the proper guidance of an experienced individual who can provide a safe space and support in integrating these experiences afterward. On the other hand, a trance drum journey provides a milder introduction, which we will present in the next exercise.

Exercise: Trance Drum Journey

A good and gentle introduction to these practices can be to listen to a trance drum journey. I have uploaded one for you on my YouTube channel at Sanyana Alaina. To get the full power of this journey, listen to the recording with headphones and use a blindfold. Lie down and take a few deep breaths. Then, consciously relax all your muscles and close your eyes. Now, let yourself sink deeper and deeper into yourself.

Imagine being in a beautiful place in nature. Look around, marvel at where you are, while at the same time listening to the drum. When the drum strokes get faster, start to follow the calling of the drum into a cave, where you will discover a tunnel going deep into the earth. Where will it lead you?

Further and further, you enter into the darkness following the beats of the drum. Until the rhythm peaks at its maximum speed, and you reach the end of the tunnel. You see a light and step out into another dimension. See what reveals itself there.

After some time, you hear the drum rhythm change again, calling you back into the tunnel. Gently, it pulls you back to the earth's surface and into the beautiful nature.

When the drum beats stop calling, you arrive back in your room. Take a deep breath and become aware of your physical form. Stay here for a moment to let your journey sink in, then, start gently moving your body. To integrate your experience, write down what you encountered, whatever it was. An image, a vision, colors, thoughts, or feelings. Trust that exactly as much and as little has shown up as it should. With practice, it will become easier for you to let yourself sink into a trance.

3. AFFIRMATIONS

Affirmations are the third most powerful way to increase, develop, and strengthen your psychic senses. Modern quantum physics proved what spiritualists had known for a long time: that it is our mind and our psyche that command and shape matter. This is known as the power of our thoughts, words, and beliefs. Whatever you expect to see in front of you will likely be what you see. Not only because you will look for it and filter out anything that is not what you are looking for—like when you scan a crowd for a familiar face and blend out all the other faces—but also because the forms you see in the outside world adapt to your perspective.

You might know this effect from dreaming when you find yourself in a particular place, think of another place, and the whole scene suddenly changes. It's common for sages and spiritual teachers to refer to our reality as a dream because it is composed the same way dreams are. Just that our waking reality functions on the illusion of time, which means that matter seems to react very slowly to the impulse of our thoughts, words, and actions. But still, it does react and form accordingly.

In other words, the more you think and expect to be a psychic, the more you will create a reality in which you are psychic. Because the cells in your body are under your direct command, whatever potential is inherent in you just needs to be activated to be used. But if you are convinced you cannot see auras, you can't. It's much like a program that is installed in your being. By rewriting the program, you suddenly unlock abilities you didn't know existed within you before because they were locked.

My best advice for you is to choose affirmations that don't seem unrealistic and out of reach from your current state. So, instead of forcing yourself to believe something that doesn't feel true to you, choose affirmations that feel like doable steps toward your goal. Instead of the full third eye-opening and psychic vision, you could start by manifesting more synchronicities and signs from the universe.

Affirm to yourself, "I am open to receiving whatever guidance the universe has for me." Instead of "I am psychic," you could start with "My psychic abilities are increasing every day." Find a truth you can believe in and affirm that. Or maybe ask yourself where in your reality you can already validate your psychic abilities and build on that. Another beautiful way to invoke your powers through affirmations is to chant them as mantras.

EXERCISE: DAILY AFFIRMATIONS

For the best results, practice these affirmations for at least 21 days and see what happens. Choose the affirmations that resonate best with you and add whatever affirmations you receive intuitively.

I can read energy and use this ability frequently.

I perceive accurate information through my psychic abilities.

I see and feel subtle energy.

My psychic abilities are getting stronger every day.

I trust my own guidance.

I am grateful for my psychic gifts.

I am a psychic empath.

You can use the different brain wave states we've discussed to make yourself even more perceptible to the effects of affirmations. Therefore, the best time to practice them is either in the morning right after waking up, when your consciousness is naturally running on alpha waves, or right as you fall asleep, moving into alpha, theta, and delta states as you drift away. In addition, you can listen to binaural beats, which stimulate your brain to enter into an alpha state.

Note: Find a recording of the most powerful affirmations for you as an empath in our meditation bundle.

4. DREAM JOURNEYING

Dreams have always been one of the great mysteries of human existence. The fact that our consciousness keeps experiencing even when our body perception goes fully unconscious proves that the world we experience isn't all there is. Through this phenomenon, we see that our pure consciousness alone is capable of experiencing other worlds, lifetimes, and stories. These worlds are realms of different densities with different sets of physical laws. That's because these are the realms of mind where our thoughts are displayed before they turn from a mental idea into physical form.

There are different levels in these dream realms. Here, we can get in contact with our own sub- and superconsciousness, which is where we will find both our shadow as well as our soul-self, and both of those aspects can communicate to us through symbols and stories.

In psychology, dreams are a very useful tool for exploring one's own shadows and subconscious stories. This is because they often reflect the core essence of our various inner parts and issues that our subconscious is currently processing. At the same time, dreams often carry messages that relate to or sometimes even prophecy events in the physical realms. Whatever we feel and experience in our dreams will also influence and shape our waking experience. A shaman sees everything in existence as a dream imagined by source consciousness. So, the more you practice conscious dreaming, the more your whole life experience becomes lucid and turns into an opportunity to manifest and create consciously.

As our body falls asleep our consciousness withdraws from the world of our waking life, our psyche stays awake and experiences the other dimensions and times that are influencing our energy field. In spaces where things are more flexible, there is no linear time, and every thought creates instantaneous results. This is why dreams are the perfect training ground for your psychic abilities.

Both your night and daydreams can be used to play around with living scenarios and adventures that help you develop your powers. Here, you can go wild, find inspiration, and create future visions that will be drawn to you in the material world. With time, what works in the mind will more likely work in the physical realm as well. In that way, dreams can be a beautiful tool to bring playfulness into the practice and get inspired about what is possible.

To start conscious dreaming, the first step is to get aware of your dream states. Dream journaling is a powerful method to enhance your dream awareness and keep track of your progress as you explore. To become more lucid in your dreams, you can supplement journaling with additional specific exercises, such as questioning whether you are awake or dreaming. This can be done throughout your day and while you are falling asleep to create a subconscious habit and increase the chances of noticing your dream state as you sleep. Another great habit to induce lucid dreaming states is so-called reality checks, like checking for a clock to see if it displays a reasonable time or trying to breathe while closing your nostrils. Since the dream realms operate on different physical laws, you will find many typical abnormalities the more you observe. Your hands might, for example, have more or less than five fingers, or the number of fingers might even change as you try to count them.

The more often you perform these tests while awake, the higher the probability that you will remember them in the dream state as well. Once you have recognized in the dream that you are dreaming, the magical training ground for your abilities can fully unfold for you.

EXERCISE: DREAM JOURNALING

To start working with your dreams intentionally, make it a habit to document them right after waking up when your brain is still running on alpha brain waves and before the door to your subconscious closes. The more you record your dreams and integrate the hidden realms of your subconscious processes, the more conscious you will become of your dreams. Then, you can start playing around. With time and disciplined journaling practice, you will find that your dreams will become more lucid and open to your own creation. This is a great way to have fun and explore the power of your mind.

5. PRACTICE

The last powerful method to strengthen your psychic senses is simple practice. Your psychic senses are like muscles that must be engaged to stay active and grow. And this can be done in all kinds of ways. Maybe you feel drawn to a particular psychic sense first that you want to focus on for a while and master before you move on to the next. Then, you can take your time with one of the following chapters and practice each exercise regularly until you feel secure in that particular psychic skill.

Generally speaking, there won't be such a thing as perfect mastery, as there will always be something new to learn or more expansion to be achieved. Still, you will notice that with practice, you will become more and more fluid in the particular sense until you start doing it intuitively.

You can start easily by playing pretend, much like we did as kids. Start playing out a reality in which you've already achieved this fluent state of "mastery" and play around with it. If it is clairvoyance you are training, try to picture the aura of the people in front of you, try to imagine what it would look like according to their emotional state, and then double-check by asking them how they are feeling. In the case of claircognizance, try to fill out the information gaps when someone is telling you a story, and then ask them about the particular detail without revealing your guess. With time, you will notice that your guesses become increasingly accurate.

What will happen is that your system starts scanning the scene for the particular information you are trying to fill out. By double-checking what you are picking up, you can get clear feedback on how your skills are developing. And especially as you start using the exercises, you will see progress much quicker than expected. Be bold, and trust in your abilities. This is the time to just do it and just be it, and never forget: life is much more like a dream than we are aware of. Experiment with that and allow yourself to play around and have fun.

EXERCISE: DREAMING YOUR HUMAN

For this exercise, take a moment to mentally take on the position of your higher self. See your character through the eyes of your soul. Decide what your human should learn and do next. From your soul's perspective, everything is possible.

You are excited to experience this dream. Life feels like a game, and you're always looking for the next opportunity to level up. And more so, you have found the cheat codes to experience anything you want in this game. Who do you wanna be? What do you want to learn? And what will be the right training to perfect your unique skills?

The more often you slip into this dream mentality, the more you will be able to apply it to your everyday perspective and remember what it's like to see life through the lens of adventure and curiosity—just like your soul.

DISCOVERING YOUR HIDDEN SENSES

While all of us have the capacity to learn and master every one of the clair senses when working with our psychic senses, you might soon notice that one or two will come much easier than the rest. That's because we all have a natural predisposition to a specific sense that we pick up easiest. You have probably noticed this fairly early in life. Maybe you had a particularly vivid imagination, prophetic dreams, invisible friends, or regular intuitive insights about other people and events.

Working with your natural psychic sense might feel especially satisfying because it yields quick results on the way to mastery. Still, you shouldn't feel like you are restricted to that sense only. You can learn whatever psychic sense you want. And in that, I will advise you to always follow the path that gives you the most joy: I know that our society teaches us many beliefs, such as: "What you can do the least, you have to learn the hardest!" Or "Only those who work hard will be successful!" Or "You must not follow the easy path that will lead you nowhere!"

But in actuality, we are born with the very gifts we need to fulfill our calling in this life. How much more joy and passion would flow if we simply focused on our strengths more and our weaknesses less? I would like to share a small personal example from my life with you: in my mid-twenties, I envisioned being a medicine woman. The strong connection to that previous life in which I had been a shaman awakened in me, and the message I received was clear: connect the old knowledge with the new and carry it into this time. And so I set out, not knowing what to expect. I started exploring my skills and training with different teachers. I got to know the spiritual scene, and something always stood out that I really didn't understand: herbalism. I got to know witches and shamans who knew so much about the plant world and who could create true miracle medicines with their means.

In the beginning, I quarreled with myself because the truth was it was very difficult for me to learn and understand the plant world. I didn't have any prior knowledge, and I forgot what I learned easily. I also didn't enjoy it when others tried to teach me—it bored me. I've always been good at following only what really touched and interested me, so I turned away from this topic.

But deep down, I was still nagging: shouldn't I actually be able to do this as a so-called medicine woman? It was my old pain and fear of not being good enough that had grown my shadow of always comparing myself to people who seemed to be further along than I was. Until one day, I sat down in meditation with this question and as so often, when you finally take the time to sit quietly, ask the question, and listen to the answer, the solution is there, quick and simple—no, I didn't need to master every aspect of the healing profession and knowledge to be a medicine woman! The message was clear: you are not here to be able to do everything in the healing field. In fact, that's not even possible. Just follow your joy and passion, and you will get everything you need and more! And so it was!

What attracts you most to learning is exactly what you need for your next step. Don't waste your valuable time with things that don't fulfill you!

Take a moment to reflect on these questions: Are there beliefs in you that tell you to do or learn certain things, even though you struggle to do so and do not feel fulfilled? If you answer yes, sit quietly and ask yourself and the universe: "How can I let go of these beliefs?" This way, you may follow the path of joy and your heart. Trust that it will lead you exactly the right way.

EXERCISE: THE ROSE GARDEN
WHICH PSYCHIC SENSE IS YOUR STRONGEST?

This exercise is great to test and get familiar with your psychic abilities, but also to check on how they've grown once you start training them regularly. Find a comfortable and undisturbed spot where you can sit down and attain a state of stillness.

Begin by attuning yourself to a meditative state, as you have learned in previous meditation exercises. Now, visualize yourself in a beautiful garden. Take in the scenery, envision the vibrant landscape, the play of light, and the vivid colors that surround you. Pay attention to the delicate flowers adorning the garden. Take a deep breath, feel the crispness of the air against your skin, and absorb the fragrant scents permeating the atmosphere. Listen to the ambient sound of your surroundings.

Now, direct your focus toward a magnificent bush adorned with striking black roses. These roses are large and glisten under the sunlight. Observe the varying shades within the petals, gently touch the leaves, and perceive the soft texture of the rose petals. Inhale deeply, taking note of the nuanced aromas of its essential oils. Now, expand your senses and feel the energy that radiates from the rose. Attempt to connect to the spirit of the plant. Notice any emotions that arise during your interaction.

Can you see the aura surrounding the rose? Can you sense any insights like visions or messages from the plant? You might notice the subtle frequency in which the rose vibrates or even hear the voice of the spirit whispering or singing. Maybe you feel inspired to talk to it? Dedicate ample time to be present with the rose, embracing the entirety of this encounter, immersing yourself fully in the experience. To finish this exercise, express your gratitude to the rose bush for facilitating this profound experience. Then, gradually return to awareness of your physical body.

Take a few moments to reflect on which sense came most naturally to you during this exercise. This sense is likely the psychic sense in which you possess a natural affinity. How easy or difficult was it for you to imagine the garden, see the aura, or perceive visions? This is your clairvoyance. Did you receive messages from the plant, have sudden inspirational thoughts, or have intuitive knowledge about the spirit or yourself in this encounter? This is your claircognizance. Could you hear the voice or frequency of the spirit, maybe even talk to it? This is your clairaudience. Could you feel the energy of the rose, feel its spirit, and notice emotions? This is your clairsentience. Pay attention to the senses you wish to develop further and train in order to enhance your ability to have vivid and profound experiences in the future.

THE PSYCHIC SENSES

WORKING WITH YOUR PSYCHIC SENSES

*I*n this chapter, we will discuss the three most common psychic senses amongst empaths besides clairsentience, which are claircognizance, clairvoyance, and clairaudience. As discussed earlier, these are governed by the upper three chakras of our bodies, which hold predominantly yang energy. With each clair sense, we will first look at the main chakra that governs this sense and then follow with the corresponding yin chakra, which balances the yang energies and enables you to put the gained insights and downloads into practice. By doing so, you will manifest wholeness into your own life.

The two senses we will not discuss further in this book are clairalience (clear smelling) and clairgustance (clear tasting). They are an extension of our senses of smell and taste and do not occur that often. These psychic abilities can show themselves, for example, in the form of visions, which one can smell and taste. For example, I once received a spiritual message from my grandfather and suddenly had his scent in my nose, which I had not smelled since he died.

When Shamans have mastered these abilities, they can, for example, already guess from the smell or taste of a plant for which healing tincture it is suitable. Some even smell when a person is sick and sense what disease it could be. These are, without a doubt, exciting abilities, but since I hardly embody them myself, I'll mention them only briefly at this point. If you resonate with these two abilities, you can experiment with them by focusing on your sense of smell or taste and become more and more fine-tuned at distinguishing smells and tastes and sensing their effect on your body. You can also focus on receiving tastes and smells during visions and meditations.

With that being said, let's dive deep into the more common clair senses.

CLAIRCOGNIZANCE
HOW TO KNOW WITH YOUR INTUITION

CROWN CHAKRA PSYCHIC SENSE: RECEIVING WISDOM

The sense of claircognizance is what connects us to our intuition and the wisdom of the universe.

It is governed by the crown chakra, known as the seat of consciousness and our direct connection to the all-knowing oversoul, our own cosmic essence. The more open the crown chakra, the clearer you will perceive your intuitive guidance. This inner voice often shows up as direct insights or sudden ideas about concepts or solutions to problems that you couldn't solve by thinking alone. That is because your oversoul, often also referred to as higher self, has a greater perspective on things and, therefore, naturally perceives a wider range of possibilities than your human mind could ever imagine. It is your connection to the all-knowing source of this universe and, therefore, has insights into any and everything that is beyond our human comprehension.

Especially in the beginning, it can be difficult to discern which idea has originated from your intuition and which has resulted from your thoughts. The strongest sign that a particular idea has come from your higher self is that it arises out of seemingly nowhere, oftentimes when you are simply relaxing and not even close to thinking about the particular subject. And when it enters your being, it usually does so with a rush of excitement and a thrill that makes you feel like a genius and inspired to put that new insight into practice immediately. These creative impulses are often accompanied by physical sensations such as goosebumps or a warm, tingling feeling in specific body parts.

You might be listening to someone talk about their problems, and without being sure of how to answer, suddenly feel the urge to give certain advice only to look into the shocked eyes of your counterpart saying: "Wow, that's exactly what I needed to hear! Thank you!" Have you ever wondered where such inspirations come from? From a shamanic perspective, you became receptive to higher consciousness by listening with your whole being.

Since the yang chakras with which we access these insights carry male energy, to perceive that energy, we have to get into our inner yin energy, our receptive mode. Yin and Yang attract each other; through the Yin energy, we can receive the Yang energy. Every time you listen to someone or watch something without letting your thoughts influence you, by simply taking in the impression, you become perceptive to whatever there truly is, and the stream of information can start.

One thing you will notice about intuitive insights is that if you don't capture them, you'll likely forget about them quickly. Similar to dreams that disappear from your short-term memory right after waking up. Intuitive insights don't originate from our conscious mind, so we cannot access them through our active perception. Another indication for intuitive guidance is that you feel led to take steps that seem illogical initially. At this point, I would like to encourage you to take these illogical steps. Intuition is so much wiser than reason will ever be and can take you to places beyond your imagination.

A possible blockage for your crown chakra connection is the shadow of mistrusting one's own intuition, which we discussed earlier. To let go of this blockage, it's important not to overthink and overanalyze the information coming through. This will build a healthy respect for your inner wisdom, which often exceeds the mind's capacity. Once you establish a solid connection to your intuition, it can guide you through difficult life decisions, show you the path of your soul growth that is most beneficial to you, and support your work as a healer through insights and downloads.

Exercise: Isolating Your Intuition

Reflect on whether there has been a recent situation where your intuition and reason have disagreed. What thoughts and feelings arose from your intuition? And what thoughts and feelings have arisen from your past and mind that have contradicted your intuition? What were the fears behind it? Now, in hindsight, see if you feel a difference between the promptings of your intuition and those of your mind. How do you perceive the difference?

For example: Which voice is louder—your intuition or your reason? What body sensations do you experience when you feel the promptings of your intuition as opposed to those of your mind? This feeling and reflection exercise trains your consciousness to recognize your intuition. As a result, you will be able to perceive that inner voice louder and earlier.

ROOT CHAKRA PSYCHIC ART: DIVINE EMBODIMENT

While the masculine insights of the yang chakras are accessed through the yin energy of receptivity, the feminine powers of the yin chakras are activated through the yang energy of active engagement. In the case of the root chakra, that is especially being aware of the body, moving, and treating it according to your highest will.

Our root chakra anchors our energy in the physical world, the human body, and the ground. It is our connection to our great Mother Earth. In order to access the high frequencies of the oversoul and bring them into the physical world, one needs to be firmly grounded on Earth and in one's body. As much as you need a good relationship with your higher self, you must nurture and take care of your human body. This part of you has a consciousness of its own and wants to be loved and treated well by you.

A well-grounded root chakra increases your sense of security and, thus, your confidence to follow your intuition. The root chakra is mainly responsible for making us feel safe in this world so that we can surrender ourselves to life with deep trust. When we are not well grounded, we carry a lot of fear in our system, which makes us very headstrong as a result. Our thoughts become too loud and drown out the voice of intuition.

You open and ground your root chakra by setting a proper self-care routine in place, developing a nurturing diet, listening to your body's physical needs, exercising regularly, and allowing for enough rest. Generally, everything that calms and relaxes your nervous system will help your body to become your most loyal vessel to perform your mission here on Earth and execute the guidance you'll access through the crown chakra.

Another way of opening and stimulating the energy flow of your root chakra is through nurturing your connection to nature, the source of all grounding energy. Especially doing our grounding meditation while being in nature and physically connected to Earth can create a huge opening in your root chakra. By doing this, you also directly stimulate your crown chakra to open up and receive higher guidance.

To understand this from a different perspective, you can picture the energies of the root chakra as the deepest feminine attributes and the energies of the crown chakra as their highest masculine counter energy. They are always connected and influence each other; both parties must be nourished accordingly to achieve a balanced state. Then they become lovers, uniting in the heart chakra, through which we can feel a deep sense of connection, bliss, and unconditional love.

Whenever you tap into the consciousness of your crown, you can, from there, cultivate the deep love your soul has for your body, and you will automatically treat yourself more tenderly throughout the day. When you go into your body consciousness, you can sense and cultivate your deep desire for union with your higher self and the source of the universe, and you will find that your body will support you in being more devoted to your practice. The more you nurture this divine connection, the more you will find that listening to your body will also tune you into hearing your intuition.

Our root chakra gets especially blocked by the shadow of people-pleasing and a lack of boundaries. As you prioritize the needs of others over your own, you signal to the body that it's 'less important', and this will ultimately cause your body to feel neglected and unsafe. To resolve that blockage, you can make a conscious decision to prioritize your body's needs over pleasing other people and practice your self-worth by setting healthy boundaries.

Exercise: Embodying Your Higher Self

To develop a grounded relationship between your higher self and your body, greet your body as you enter it first thing in the morning, right after waking up from sleep. Check-in with your body, like you would with a close friend or lover. Ask how it feels today and what it wants to do. Does it want to go for a walk? Get barefoot on the grass? Does it want to play or dance or sing? What food does it need today? When planning your day, make a conscious decision to consider what your body needs, and keep checking in with your body throughout the day. Talk to it as your higher self and notice the difference it will make in your life.

SUPERPOWER: LIVING AN INTUITIVE LIFE

The superpower is the combined power of both chakras when the yin and yang aspects create a harmonious flow. When these powerful chakras are aligned and working together, life will become an intuitive flow, always connected to the highest consciousness yet firmly rooted in the present. You will awaken to a sense of wonder by what you will find around you as you explore this divine creation and experience the world through the eyes of your soul.

Once the accuracy of your intuitive insights has been proven often enough, your body and mind will be trained to follow these hints by default, saving precious energy that might've gone into overthinking previously. You will be anchored in a deep peace and inner calm. Your whole life will become an embodiment of the highest divine will, which will make it possible for you to receive all the magic and wonders around you that are just waiting for you to open up to them. You will experience a deep sense of connection and peace that you likely have never felt before.

Sounds too good to be true? You'll only ever know by trying! :)

EXERCISE: CREATING SPACE TO CONNECT TO YOUR HIGHER SELF
The connection to your higher self is like any other connection in your life, a relationship that needs to be nurtured in order to grow. If you want to have an intimate bond with your higher self—and therefore to your source of intuition and connection with this whole existence—you need to create space

and time in which you are present with your essence.

This can be done by creating a sacred space in your home where you can meditate, meet, and pray, practice your psychic abilities, and receive guidance. Set the space up as if you were about to hang out with your favorite friend—a comfy zone to relax and let go. Then, create a routine of spending time there. The more consistently you invest in this relationship, the more you will notice your higher self showing up in your everyday reality to pass downloads, comments, and even inside jokes. You might be surprised at the divine's excellent humor.

CLAIRVOYANCE
YOUR SENSE OF VISION

THIRD EYE CHAKRA PSYCHIC SENSE: RECEIVING VISIONS

Have you ever noticed that you can see without opening your eyes? Every time you close your eyes and go down memory lane to replay a situation of the past, you see visual images in your mind. These images already express your psychic ability because you perceive them with your psyche as a form of inner vision. This inner vision is called internal clairvoyance. With a fully opened third eye, you perceive images and visions beyond the physical world, from the subtle realms and your soul.

They show up as sudden flashes of inspiration, where you seem to get the full, in-detail picture of a random moment without prior warning and with seemingly nothing to have triggered it. In other situations, you might listen to someone else's thoughts and suddenly see a whole idea in the form of a vision in front of your inner eye. An idea you haven't puzzled together but instead became open to perceive. Such inspired downloads from our surroundings can be received through all the clair senses. While intuitive insights perceived from the crown chakra will have a more conceptual nature, when perceived through our third eye, they take the form of visuals, colors, or patterns.

You might perceive information about the nature of problems or possible solutions as future visions. Your inner eye sees beyond the limitations of our physical world and even beyond time, as we can see in the case of memory. This is also what the stereotypical concept of the clairvoyant fortune teller points toward. In reality, these people see possibilities that can be manifested, depending on whether the subjects continue their current energetic direction or change their course.

Not only does your inner eye perceive beyond the average human range, but external clairvoyance typically shows up as seeing the phenomenon in your surroundings that most others don't see. They might seem like hallucinations at first, but they usually have a cause or reference in the energetical dimension of our world. They appear as shadows or light beams, radiating color or even auric fields surrounding people and objects.

What blocks this chakra and the sense of clairvoyance is the shadow of unhealthy attachment, especially toward other people, such as toxic relationships. Since they thrive on the habit of diluting themselves by seeing through heavy filters of likes and dislikes, the more you are attached to seeing someone or something in a certain light, the more you will project onto the outside world, and the less accurate truth you will see. The same happens when the savior shadow is active. An open third eye sees a person as a whole, including their trauma, energy field, and soul. When the savior shadow is active, the trauma bond is so strong that it overshadows all other fields. We no longer perceive this person's greatness or the soul that chose its path in this way. We only see the person as helplessly lost in their trauma.

To start seeing clearly, you have to look at circumstances the way they are and try to see beyond the filters your shadow might project onto a situation. Your inner eyes will open when you dare to look at the truth and resist trying to change it or look through tainted glasses to avoid what you don't want to see. Another way of strengthening your psychic sense of clairvoyance is to daydream whenever you feel inspired. Start by visualizing possible futures, and go into as much detail as possible about the places and surroundings you want to be in.

The following exercise is a useful tool to train your sense of clairvoyance. Don't forget to have fun with it as you experiment.

EXERCISE: THE CANDLE FLAME MEDITATION

This is a powerful exercise to open your third eye and activate your inner vision; to do this exercise, light a candle and place it right before you. Find a comfortable position and rest your gaze on the candle flame. Look at the flame for about 1 minute, or until your eyes start tearing or it gets uncomfortable. Then close your eyes for 2 minutes and watch the candle flame before your inner eye until it fades away. Try to bring it back and recreate the impression of the flame in as much detail as possible. Then open your eyes and repeat. Do this for up to 15 minutes or until your eyes get tired. You will notice that your inner visions and dreams will become more vivid and clear over time; this exercise is like a cleanse for the inner vision.

You can incorporate tea into the ritual whenever you have enough time and feel inspired to hold a sacred ceremony. Green tea, for example, is very suitable. Thank the tea spirit for being with you, and think of the energy you would like to give into this ritual. Perhaps you are asking for a specific vision or want to be open to whatever the tea will show you. Feel the tea spreading through you, relaxing your body and helping you to open your energetic field. Then, look into the candle and meditate. Watch for what comes up and see if you can sink deeper with your eyes closed or open. You can perform this ceremony in silence or with music.

Note: Find a supportive playlist for this exercise in our free Spotify bundle.

EXERCISE: AURIC VISION

Activating your auric vision is a great way to train your external clairvoyance since it requires you to readjust your visual focus and range of your vision. Seeing someone's aura means seeing their surrounding energy field, which takes on a different intensity and color depending on their mood and energy flow. This exercise works best with a partner but can also be performed alone with a mirror. If you have a partner, place them in front of a white wall or alternatively stand with your back to a white wall and look into the mirror.

Focus your gaze on the point in between the eyebrows of either yourself or your partner. Keep your eyes locked in that position, and start playing with the focus of your gaze. Concentrate on the outer lines of your peripheral vision instead of the middle of your focus point. Look at the frame more than the content, and you will notice that the face in front of you will darken until only a bright glow surrounds it. This is the aura.

Now, try to hold this vision for as long as possible. You can close your eyes and observe the shadow impression in your inner eye. Experiment with that vision, play around, and you will become more receptive whenever you do it. With training, you will be able to tune into this auric vision much quicker and more intuitively. This new ability will greatly support your work as a healer as it enables you to spot energy leaks, imbalances, or toxic energies such as suppressed emotions and thereby also track the progress of your work.

SACRAL CHAKRA PSYCHIC ART: CREATING WORLDS

Once you open the energy flow of your third eye chakra, you will notice that your daydreams and fantasy worlds will become more vivid and inspired. You might find that you get lost in your mind space more often, and here, it's again important for you to be firmly grounded in your physical body and the material world.

Opening your third eye chakra will help you receive divinely inspired visions, but it is your sacral chakra that you need to create and attract those possibilities into the physical realm. And that's where the real adventure starts: when you are able to recreate your fantasies and live them out in the human world.

The sacral chakra is the yin chakra that corresponds to your third eye and balances its powers. It's the seat of our passions, emotions, and creative energies. It is located in our pelvis area right below the navel and governs the sexual organs, our seat of creation. This chakra is about expressing and bringing ideas to life, but not only that — it's also the seat of our desires. Here, we'll get the energetic fuel to manifest our visions. A vibrant sacral chakra makes us magnetic and calls in all the right people, places, and opportunities.

It's where our abundant life energy and vitality reside. It governs our attractiveness as well as how we create with others and the whole universe. While the root chakra is linked with the body's safety, the sacral chakra is all about the pleasure of our human form. It thrives when we engage in all types of movement, such as painting, dancing, singing, and physical exercise.

This chakra gets mainly blocked by shame and guilt, especially around our sexual energies, which are our creative fuel. If you, for example, experienced a lot of shame around moving or touching your body, as many in our society do, chances are that your natural sacral flow is somewhat blocked. If this is the case, it can lead to the shadow of escaping into fantasy worlds. Here, it is important to take the inspirations gained through one's visualizations and to express them as much as possible, either by journaling about them, painting them, or enacting them as if they were already part of your reality!

To open this chakra, engage in everything that gives your body pleasure and feel that pleasure entirely. This means conscious sexuality, both with a partner and yourself, but also seeking pleasure in everything you do.

Every daily activity can bring us pleasure. While washing dishes, you can, for example, focus on the warm water on your hands, the soothing scent of the soap, and the satisfaction of seeing the dishes become clean and shiny. Or, when going for a walk, you can take the time to appreciate the beauty of nature around you, the fresh air filling your lungs, and the gentle movement of your body. While cooking a meal, savor the aromas, textures, and flavors of the ingredients. Engage your senses fully and enjoy the process of creating something delicious. During a workout or exercise routine, focus on the physical sensations of your body, the rush of endorphins, and the sense of accomplishment as you push yourself to new limits. When engaging in a creative activity like painting, writing, or playing an instrument, immerse yourself fully in the process, allowing your imagination to flow freely and enjoying the act of self-expression.

Remember, finding pleasure in all the things you do can enhance your overall enjoyment and bring a sense of fulfillment to your daily life. In everything we do, we can consciously connect with pleasure and thus involve our Sacral Chakra.

EXERCISE: INTUITIVE MOVEMENT MEDITATION

Dancing of any sort will help you open the energy flow of your sacral chakra, especially in the form of intuitive movement, as it is a way to tap into whatever your body truly longs for at that moment. It is a way to feel your body as it naturally moves and thereby connects you to your deeper body consciousness.

For this exercise, choose one of your favorite dance tracks. It has to be something that gets your blood cooking and your body ready to move. Choose a space in which you are undisturbed, turn up the music, and let your body flow however it likes. Don't worry about feeling stiff in the beginning; just try to encourage yourself to let loose and experiment with how your body wants to move.

The most amazing part is that you will find that the more you tune into your body consciousness, the more receptive you will become to higher guidance and ideas. Dance is a great practice to invoke these energies, especially when it includes moving the hips. These are the moments of genius epiphanies and magical synchronicities. Just try and enjoy!

SUPERPOWER: MANIFESTATION

When your third eye and sacral chakra work in harmony, your life will become a flow of creative energy. Your imagination will become a powerful inspiration for your desires to create and attract whatever you have visualized. Your open third eye chakra will enable you to see beyond the present and envision future possibilities, triggering desire in your creative center, which helps you attract the people, places, and opportunities you need to make that vision come true. Together, they create worlds!

When both of these powerful psychic skills are active, you will feel deeply connected to higher universal guidance, receiving inspired visions, and you will be able to manifest those inspirations effortlessly and playfully. The world will become your playground, inviting you to co-create with the highest divine consciousness and let yourself be surprised by what an amazing adventure your life will turn into. Synchronicities will start to increase; your whole reality field will interact with that new enlivening energy. You will learn to see what's really for you and follow the divine's call that will guide you to visions and possibilities far beyond your imagination.

EXERCISE: SEX MAGIC RITUAL

One beautiful way to combine these powers practically is sex magic. Our orgasmic energy is the most powerful source of energy available to us; it is the energy that creates life and from which we all originated. You can consciously use it to create and manifest what you desire, and to also connect more deeply with your own body, let new beliefs flow into you, or any kind of personal healing you desire. The important thing is that you stay open to how and when your desire will be fulfilled. Let the universe surprise you with how you will be guided to what's in your highest interest.

Also, note that it's not about having an orgasm. It is true that orgasm is a moment of powerful, energetic release that can be a beautiful part of this ritual. But we should not strive for it because the really important thing is to deeply enjoy the encounter with ourselves and to be present in every moment. It's about letting pleasure flow through your veins as freely as possible, without expectations or any need to perform. Simply let the pleasure renew your cells and leave your body and energy field younger, healthier, and fresher.

1. Begin this exercise by meditating on your desired future vision; see it in front of your third eye, with as many details as possible.

2. Now, start moving either with your partner or by yourself. Touch your body lovingly. Awaken your life energy, longing, and passion by connecting to your sacral chakra. You can support this by infusing the air with a scent

you like. Deep breathing, conscious relaxation, and listening to your body will support you in being fully connected.

3. Reconnect with your vision, feel your future, and what it will be like to live it. How do you feel there? Express those feelings in your movements. Enjoy your body, move with your future like you are celebrating it, and feel the deep pleasure running through your body, fueling your future vision with vitality. Be wild, soft, slow, crazy - whatever you like!

4. Let the pleasure and joy of this state grow ever greater, and once you hit a peak of euphoria and passion, raise your heart and arms to release your vision toward Heaven, sending all of the beautiful feelings into the universe.

5. Now spread your arms wide open to receive an answer from that time and dimension of the universe where your desired future already exists.

Receive her; she is here now. Stay in her presence—that feeling of already being your future version—for as long as you can. Feel that she is already in you. You are blessed!

6. Lastly, thank the universe for allowing its divine energy to flow through you.

7. Repeat this process of sending up and receiving as many times as you like.

Note: If you feel shame coming up, know that it's your inner sacral blockage, and you can use that opportunity to release that blockage by consciously giving in to your movements. Another helpful tool is loudly affirming: "I let go of all old shame! I deserve to feel pleasure in my body!"

CLAIRAUDIENCE
YOUR SENSE OF HEARING

THROAT CHAKRA PSYCHIC SENSE: RECEIVING SOUND

Clairaudience describes the ability to hear beyond the average physical human range and is governed by the throat chakra. As the name suggests, this chakra is located in the throat area and rules over our ears and vocal cords, which means it is in charge of how we perceive and create sound.

For many, the gift of clairvoyance can show up as general noise sensitivity or the ability to hear what others don't hear. But especially for empaths, this can mean hearing other people's thoughts, sometimes as loud as their own. Unconscious empaths might even mistake these thoughts for their own and struggle to hear and detect their inner voices when they are around others. In those cases, it helps to work on your sense of self and on your boundaries.

The throat chakra is strengthened by speaking the truth and listening beyond the ego's filters. The more truth you cultivate around you, the more sensitive you will become to hearing things as they are, and the less you are distracted by illusions, the deeper you can listen to what's truly being said.

When our throat chakra is in harmony, we speak harmony. Anything that is disharmonious will feel very uncomfortable and alarming to someone sensitive to sound, especially to those who are clairaudient. As a clairaudient, you might also be able to tune into the sound of things and notice whether they swing in harmony or where there are blocks somewhere in the field—a skill that can help you greatly in your work as a healer.

You can hear what is true and what is a lie because you sense the energy that underlies the spoken word, and you become sensitive to changes in the tone and sound of the voice. You might notice that you hear people's subconscious voices, too, and you also sense when there is a deeper meaning behind what is being said, even things the speaker is unaware of.

The energy channels around this chakra can get wounded if one is prohibited from speaking their truth. But there are also ways in which we create blockages ourselves. This could, for example, be by choosing not to speak our truth, maybe in an attempt to deceive others or for lack of boundaries, which tempts us to sugarcoat things and even lie to make people feel more comfortable.

It could also happen through gossiping about others or through mindless complaining, thereby denying our own power to change a situation. In these cases, the energy flow becomes stagnant and eventually stops. Another cause for a throat chakra blockage can be talking too much without ever listening or listening without ever talking since all energy flows strive to be balanced by nature. What goes out must flow back in, and vice versa.

So, if you have trouble making progress with your clairaudient abilities, you might want to take a closer look at your throat chakra. When this chakra is open and healed, you perceive sounds with clarity and are generally much better understood by your surroundings. Your singing voice will improve to touch yourself and others on a deep level, and as your voice becomes sweet and pure, like a fountain of truth, more people will listen to you and seek you out for advice and guidance.

To develop clear hearing abilities, you need to make listening a conscious habit. When doing so, try not to focus on your own thought stream but instead notice and isolate as many acoustic details as possible. The more you listen, the more sounds your mind will register as it extends its habitual perception range to fit your new interests and curiosities.

There are many different ways to open your throat chakra further. One very simple but effective way is to make it a habit to hum or sing throughout your day and as often as possible. Learn a new instrument, experiment with different types of sounds, and notice how sounds and noise make you feel. To stimulate the energy flow, you can also try screaming at the top of your lungs (even if just into a pillow) or practice yoga poses and breathing exercises specifically for the throat chakra and, of course, speak your own truth as often as possible.

EXERCISE: LISTENING CLOSER

Sitting in meditation and listening to silence is a great way to increase auditory sensitivity, as this will cleanse and sharpen your sound sensors. At first, you might feel like there is nothing to discover in the absence of noise. Still, with time, you'll notice that the deeper you surrender to it, the more fullness you'll find in the silence. This will reveal a stream of dynamic information dancing around you that is always ready to hand you whatever information or insight you need at any point.

EXERCISE: LISTENING TO SACRED MANTRAS

Listening to sacred music is another beautiful way of strengthening and developing your clairaudience. This can be your favorite mantra or an instrumental that speaks to you; something you can listen to without getting bored too quickly. Since music is a powerful form of communication that programs our subconscious mind, you want to be conscious about what kind of lyrics and frequencies you are feeding to your subconscious and what they are informing you about.

Choose one specific song that you will focus on and listen to it a few times in a row. Notice all the different instruments and melodies coming together in harmony, then choose one particularly subtle instrument, like a background drum or flute, and start isolating it in your mind. With practice, you will notice how the sound you isolated will become more recognizable and almost seem louder when you listen to the song again. And that's because you have successfully expanded your range of hearing.

When working with a mantra, singing along can greatly enhance this practice, as it will strengthen your voice and balance your listening and speaking abilities.

Note: Find a playlist with our favorite mantras in our free Spotify bundle.

SOLAR PLEXUS CHAKRA PSYCHIC ART:
NARRATING YOUR OWN STORY

The yin chakra that will help you balance any clairaudient downloads is the solar plexus chakra, the seat of our sense of individuality and willpower—our force and strength to push through obstacles and stand up for our own ideals and beliefs. It is the energy center that enables us to know our boundaries, thoughts, aspirations, and wishes, and it gets strengthened the more we speak up for ourselves.

As we've discovered in the previous pages, clairaudient abilities weaken if the connected yin chakra is blocked. This is why strengthening your solar plexus chakra will directly increase your ability to hear and especially express the truth you perceive. It helps us to be secure in ourselves and our truth, which enables us to become more open to other truths, as they can no longer unsettle or unbalance us and, therefore, don't pose a threat to us anymore.

If this chakra is out of alignment, we aren't clear about our identity and purpose of existence and, therefore, lack confidence and clarity in knowing and speaking our truth. We struggle to discern between the beliefs of others and our own and tend to adapt to what our environment suggests rather than listen to our inner voice. This also creates an energy blockage in the throat chakra since you can only vocalize a truth that you are aware of and confident about.

Without that confidence, your speech won't have any power and will likely not be heard or taken seriously by others. An imbalance in that area, therefore, shows up as a lack of boundaries and an unclear sense of self. It often comes with the shame of being not good enough and constantly questioning and doubting yourself and your identity.

To open the energy flow of your solar plexus chakra, spend time getting to know yourself. Prioritize yourself and consciously listen to your heart and body. You could, for example, make it a practice to repeat your favorite affirmations in front of the mirror several times a day or do interviews with yourself.

Who are you, independent of what others see in you? What can you see in yourself? What do you want to embody? What are your values, and what do you want to stand for? What is it you like about yourself? What do you think others cannot see or accept about yourself that you want to own with more confidence? Start a video diary or write a daily journal if you feel inspired.

EXERCISE: DATE YOURSELF

This exercise will help you get in touch with yourself the way you would get in touch with a friend of yours. Take yourself out to do something nice and consciously listen to your thoughts for a whole night. If you don't like going out alone, you can also try sitting in front of a mirror to have dinner with yourself. Just you, your favorite music, your favorite drink, food, or whatever it is that you need to enjoy yourself.

Be curious about yourself and show interest in understanding your deepest wishes, desires, hopes for the future, needs and aspirations, boundaries, and weaknesses. Show interest in yourself the way you would with someone you're attracted to. And with time, you will notice the more you open up to yourself, the more you will fall in love with this beautiful individual who's always been closest to you yet has been overlooked and taken for granted too often. In this exercise, I ask you to focus all your love and affection on yourself. And this self-love will, with time, encourage you to keep up your boundaries the way you would protect the boundaries of your most loved ones.

SUPERPOWER: SPEAKING AND PERCEIVING TRUTH

With both your solar plexus chakra and throat chakra aligned, you will be able to embody your authentic self unapologetically and become a powerful receptor and distributor of harmonious sound frequencies. This can be through your speech, singing, or even your harmonious presence. You will be gifted with the ability to heal people with words and sounds by speaking the truth they might've been unable to see, by singing sounds that harmonize their system, or sending them messages from their soul and spirit allies. Over time, you will also learn to identify imbalances and blockages within yourself or others just by listening. A voice can reveal areas where access is limited and where certain themes or even traumas reside. This will also enable you to spot lies more intuitively, just from listening to someone.

With your awakening abilities, you will discover that your voice is an effective tool for healing and self-expression, and the more you open yourself to it, the more powerful it will become.

EXERCISE: CHANTING HEALING SOUNDS

In this exercise, we will engage in a creative and intuitive practice of singing healing sounds. Shamans have used sound since the beginning of time to get into trance states, connect to the spirits, and perform healing rituals. Because they knew that sounds are the most basic form of vibrational information and have the ability to touch us very close to our core.

Our hearts and souls. Put into a rhythm, it creates patterns or frequencies that create all of Earth's phenomena. Therefore, sound is one of the purest forms of vibration we can access. When exposed to sound, our whole being, every cell, starts to vibrate at the frequency of that sound. Sound healing practices use that phenomenon by exposing our bodies to specific harmonies, which correct energy imbalances by informing the cells to vibrate in harmony again.

There are no rules or guidelines to follow in this exercise. Simply let yourself make sounds, whether it's tones, noises, or words, and see where they lead you. Your voice will guide you to different places depending on where you are in your personal journey. It may sing of pain, fear, happiness, or connection. It can summon specific energies or release old energies from within you. The key is to let go of any preconceived notions about how you should sound or sing and allow your voice to express whatever is present in the moment. Even unpleasant sounds may emerge. These sounds can help break through limitations and allow energy to flow freely. Over time, you will find that your chanting becomes more diverse and multifaceted.

Find a quiet space and take a few deep breaths. Closing your eyes can help you surrender more deeply and observe where your voice takes you. Alternatively, looking into a mirror can strengthen your connection with your current self. Instruments such as drums or rattles can provide additional support.

Enter a state of deep meditation and allow yourself to follow your impulses. Let yourself be surprised by the tones, melodies, and sounds that emerge from within you. Notice how the energy in your body shifts through your vocalization and let your voice become a source of medicine, harmonizing your being and facilitating healing.

USING YOUR PSYCHIC SENSES TO WORK WITH SPIRITS

One beautiful way of using your psychic senses is to call in spirits to help and support your work. It's a beautiful practice that combines the strengths and qualities of the different chakras. It's where it all comes together. Depending on how a specific spirit prefers to communicate or which channel is most open in your system, they might appear as audible voices or intuitive impulses to speak.

During my work, I regularly experience flushes of inspiration when I notice that a specific entity wants to communicate a specific healing frequency to a ritual. This often comes out in a language that I neither speak nor would be able to repeat in retrospect; you may have heard of it under the term light language.

Many empaths might also feel the presence of a spirit in the room—energetically or physically. Shamans often go into a trance to call forth or invoke a specific being or spirit to take over and lend its strength and wisdom. This powerful technique enables you to channel energies beyond yourself, for example, when you want to channel healing for a whole group of people and wish for extra support.

This technique takes firm grounding and centering in your heart space. You need to feel good about what you're doing and be able to trust in spirit, so take it slow when inviting spirits into your work. Whenever you work with spirits, communicate your needs and boundaries clearly, just as you would do with a human that you invite into your space.

PSYCHIC ABILITIES AND PSYCHOSIS

One thing I would like to note is that generally, with every extra sensory perception skill, you should always only go as far as feels comfortable and secure for you. In the next chapter, we will look into methods to protect yourself from overwhelming psychic energy and equip you with whatever you need in case you feel uncomfortable by the psychic intake. Since the phenomenon of perceiving sensory information beyond the average human range, such as visuals or voices, can be unsettling, here are a few words on feeling like you are going "crazy."

In a mysterious world like ours, I find it difficult to call anything a hallucination that another person experiences contrary to common perception. I do, however, agree with the definition in psychology that a dysfunction or disorder is the case when the subject, by their sensory experience, is somehow hindered in their everyday tasks and experiences a decrease in life quality to the point that life becomes overwhelming and therefore needs help. In other words, I see receiving more than the average person only as a problem if it elicits fear in you, the energies are malevolent, or even threatening toward yourself or others.

If you feel unsafe or bothered in any way, it is usually a sign of being ungrounded. If even our discussed grounding practices won't help, don't hesitate to consult a trustworthy shaman, therapist, or other support. Your psychic abilities should never haunt you but always enhance your experience.

THE EMPOWERED EMPATH

*N*ow that we have examined all the different ways in which you can enhance and use your psychic powers, it's time for us to talk about the proper spiritual cleansing and charging routine you will need to keep your energy channels open and ensure you don't lose energy when working with your spiritual gifts. Especially when doing energy work on others, you want to have tools to keep your field clear of any unwanted energies that might attach themselves to you.

HOW TO PROTECT YOUR ENERGY

Before we look at the different tools for energetic protection, I want to say a few words about protection from unwanted energies, such as bad wishes directed toward you or even shadow energies of others that you get exposed to without being able to withdraw. I often get those questions: What do we do when we feel the need to protect ourselves from outside negative energies? It seems to me that many spiritualists carry a lot of fear around being somehow influenced by unwanted external energies. While there are ways to create a field of protection, I think the first important step to prevent any possible harm done to your energy field is to get out of the mindset of fearing being overpowered by outside forces.

In actuality, any outside influence can only affect you as much as you allow it to. As an empowered empath, you need to be aware of your own role in what you attract and what can affect you. Generally, we need more awareness around the fact that to be affected by a frequency, one has to be receptive to it. That goes for all energy sent your way, both negative and positive. You have to be open and receptive for your own blessings to reach you, and the same goes for harmful energy. This is why belief plays such a great role in our fate. Out of all the possible energies surrounding you, you are precisely aware of the ones that confirm your convictions. Therefore, you draw them in; you resonate with them. So, when it comes to ill intentions, you have all the authority to decide what energies you are receptive to.

To make this point clear, imagine you call someone's home. You call repeatedly, but the person has gone into their garden and decided never to answer the phone. You won't be able to tell them anything whether you want to or not. It's the same with energy; if you send energy to someone who is not ready to receive it, it will never reach them. That is why, in energy sessions, it is so important to invite participants to open themselves up to receive a certain energy. If they don't, much less energy will be able to reach them—sometimes even no energy at all. It is also important to remember that the conscious system can support something, but the subconscious decides whether it wants to absorb the energy or not. So, to gain full authority over what you are receptive to, you may also need to address your subconscious.

Using our telephone example, you can picture it like this: you are in the garden because you made a conscious decision not to answer the phone. You know it's your grandma trying to make you feel guilty for not being a perfect grandchild, and any attempts of respectful communication have been futile in the past. You decide for yourself that you are worth more than this energy. You still hear the ringing; your system senses someone trying to reach you. If there's no unresolved issue around guilt in your system, you will be able to let it ring and continue to stay focused on your beautiful garden. Your subconscious is at peace, and the energy cannot find a docking point.

But suppose you have an unresolved issue around this topic, for example, an old wound of guilt from your childhood and the resulting belief telling you that you should always answer when grandma calls. In that case, the energy will reach you, and you might start feeling guilty even though you didn't pick up the phone. Suddenly, you can no longer stay focused on your garden. Your subconscious has soaked up the energy and connected it to an old belief.

So, if you feel like someone is sending "bad" energies, then your conscious self most likely doesn't want to pick them up, and you try to push them away, distract them away, or whatever your strategy is. But if that energy hits a sore spot in your subconscious, you will absorb it. You can tell whether it hits a point by whether you are triggered or not. Are you calm and centered, and just realize that someone wants to contact you with an energy you are no longer the addressee of? In that case, you are not triggered. The energy does not find a docking point in your subconscious, so it cannot reach you. Then, you remain in deep peace and simply send the energy firmly but lovingly back to its source.

Or does this energy trigger an emotional response in you? Do you get frantic, nervous, angry, or even anxious and desperate? Then, the energy has found a docking point in your subconscious, and no matter how hard you try to distract it away, it has already reached you. But that's not bad news. On the contrary, once you are aware of it, you can use the "negative" energy that is sent your way to heal more deeply. If it finds a docking point in your system, that means nothing more than that you have an undiscovered and unhealed wound there that wants to be seen. As soon as you become aware of this wound and feel it through, the energy from the outside is automatically drained, and you emerge from the situation more whole and healed than you were before.

And this goes for all unwanted energies, whether they are sent to you intentionally or unintentionally. The best protection against any energy is always to clear your system, especially your shadow of its frequency. To become so filled with your own energy of harmony that low vibrational energies simply don't resonate with your energy field and, therefore, cannot affect you. So, most often, we find that if we need to protect ourselves frequently, it is old, unhealed wounds and shadows that have weakened our energy field and are ready to be released and healed. Only when we heal those wounds and address the trauma can we elevate beyond the need to shield ourselves from possible dangers and become fully empowered. Then unwanted vibrations can't mess with us.

As an example, one common theme I see a lot in trauma work is the encounter with someone else's demon during shamanic rituals, meditation, or breathing exercises. I experienced multiple cases where clients went so deep in our trauma work sessions that they could connect to a deep subconscious shadow voice and express it so authentically that other participants felt like they saw a demon leave this person. This usually creates a little shock moment for people who are present, especially if it's their first encounter with such an experience. But once they see that the space is still being held and someone with calm energy is with the person and supporting them, most can simply shake off that energy and refocus on themselves.

In some cases, individuals feel so deeply disturbed by what they have witnessed that they are suddenly convinced the demon has now taken possession of them instead. Whenever that happens, I direct the client's awareness back to themselves by asking whether they can recognize this demon as a pain they were already familiar with. And this is usually what creates such profound self-realization and change in perspective that the need for protection or even exorcism, as some shamans will recommend, is simply unnecessary.

This means the person realizes that the demon didn't overtake them but merely existed in them for a long time as an unconscious and suppressed pain and got activated, brought to the surface by that outside trigger. In truth, the pain just wanted to be seen, acknowledged, and loved. Whenever this happened, and I checked in with both clients after these incidents, I found that both had experienced the same or very similar kinds of traumas.

Every demon is a form of deep pain that starts creating stories in the subconscious and coloring our perspective from behind the scenes. This pain usually wants to be seen, loved, healed, and released. The more we reject that pain in ourselves and others, the louder it will get and the more haunted and victimized we will feel until we realize that it has always been in our power to take care of that suppressed trauma that left us vulnerable to other people's pain. From a healed perspective, you will celebrate seeing someone else unleash their inner demon because you see the freedom that comes with releasing such deep pain instead of feeling threatened that the pain will hit you next.

Another example could be facing situations where our insecurities leave us vulnerable to losing energy to outside forces. You may find yourself in a situation with someone whose energy makes you feel uncomfortable, and you feel a strong need to protect yourself. What you need more than a magical shield against this energy in this situation is self-worth and the courage to maintain your own boundaries; for example, demand more distance or just walk away.

In my work as a coach, I have encountered many clients who wanted to use protection to stay in unhealthy environments. That will never work in the long run. What is needed in those cases is the deep healing of recognizing that one is worthy of a different environment, for example, a different job, as well as the faith that there is a better possibility if we open ourselves to it.

Healing is, therefore, always the strongest and highest protection against unwanted energies because there won't be soil for any negative seed to grow. But since healing a specific docking point is a process that takes time, until you've reached there, you will need tools to handle situations in which you might be confronted with energies that you just don't want to allow into your field at that particular moment. You have the right to choose so.

Even when we have healed our self-worth, there might be days when we feel too exhausted to hold up our natural boundaries or when we cannot just leave the environment. In these cases, the energy protection tools we will discuss in this chapter can be useful to help you feel safe. Whenever you feel like you need to use them, just check in with yourself later and address the core issue if needed, as we did in the exercise 'Finding Your Hidden Stories.'

If you don't, you'll just keep attracting situations and people that resonate with that wound and will need constant protection. It is important to be aware that holding up energetic protection takes energy and, over time, can keep you from experiencing the love and the fullness of life you deserve. When you feel safe in yourself and are fully connected to your heart energy and the light of your soul, you will notice that there is no need for protection, just a need to feel whole.

In general, it is always good to remember that from a soul perspective, the challenges you meet in life are not here to victimize you but to give you a chance to grow stronger. We didn't come here to experience the world from a high tower, shielded and guarded against everything that could possibly harm us, because the more we shield ourselves, the more we lock ourselves in. On the other hand, having an open heart is such a beautiful way of experiencing life and this world through awe and wonder, which is also your greatest potential as an empath. Existing in the power of your own heart center, where nothing can ever really harm you, protected by the eternal light of our universal source herself: Love.

From the perspective of a shamanic healer, your greatest fear, and therefore your greatest opponent, brings you the greatest possible strength by inspiring you to face your limitations and grow beyond yourself.

Many shamanic traditions report initiatory dream journeys or trance experiences in which they faced their worst fear, for example, in the form of a monster, which later turned out to become their most powerful spirit animal. Going through this dismembering process will force the prospect to face their fear of the unknown and even death. The monster could challenge the prospective shaman to fight and conquer it, and at other times, the shaman must willingly let the spirit eat them. These initiations usually mean the beginning of the shaman's calling to heal—like the final exam to reach the next level of soul growth. After the process, the previously most feared spirit becomes the shaman's greatest ally, giving them great power.

Therefore, shamanic traditions can be a beautiful way to show us how our greatest fears can become our greatest strengths and assets. And how especially those energies that we might at first feel frightened of often come in our greatest interest.

FOUR WAYS TO PROTECT YOURSELF FROM UNWANTED ENERGIES

1. STRENGTHEN YOUR OWN ENERGY FIELD

So, as mentioned in the previous section, the best protection is always to keep your own energy field as strong and radiant as possible. As a result, you will notice that you won't attract as many negative people and situations anymore, and even if you do encounter them, they simply cannot affect your field. When your cup is filled with love, overflowing even, it is much harder to add anything to it.

It will keep purifying itself through the infinite stream of love from the source. One of the easiest ways to do that is to bless each chakra with the intent and emotions you want to experience. If you have a specific weak spot, theme, or blockage in any of the chakras, you can take that chakra and focus on blessing it frequently until you see the changes you want.

EXERCISE: BLESSING THE CHAKRAS

Find a quiet spot to meditate and ensure you are comfortable. Connect to your breath and become present with yourself. As you are watching yourself breathe, become aware of how all inhales and exhales vibrate through your whole energy field. Feel into that field and bless it with light and love. Now, one after another, starting at your root chakra, feel where the chakra is located in your body and then feel where the chakra is located in your energy field.

Send love both into that field and your body simultaneously. Sit with each chakra for as long as you like and sense what the field reveals. It is possible that old emotions or beliefs pop up; in that case, simply acknowledge and release them, thanking them for the lessons they brought. Once you're done with the individual chakras, you can connect to the energy field surrounding you and use your breath to infuse that field with the energy of each chakra. With practice, you will notice that your energy will become more dominant and overpower any low vibrational energy around you.

2. CREATING A GOLDEN BALL OF PEACE AND LIGHT AROUND YOU

This exercise is a great solution if you find yourself in a situation where you need immediate protection, for example, when you are energetically exhausted and someone else starts pouring their worries into you. In these situations, you might find yourself unable to withdraw your energy or create a boundary, but you can use this exercise to create a protective golden light ball around your whole energy field. That way, you can radiate the highest frequency into your energy field and shield off any lower frequency you might need protection from at that very moment.

EXERCISE: GOLDEN BALL OF PROTECTION

To make this exercise even more effective, I recommend starting by centering and grounding yourself, as we did in Chapter 3. Then, turn your awareness inward and visualize a golden light starting in your heart center. By inhaling deeply, expand that light ball as big as you can. Feel that ball filled with the unconditional love of the universe, holding you like a caring mother. Keep breathing and expanding that light until it is big enough to hold your whole energy field, knowing that you are held and comforted by Mother Earth and the highest universal love. Always.

3. CALLING IN A SPIRIT ANIMAL FOR SUPPORT

Whenever you need extra support or find yourself in a situation where you feel particularly lonely, you can always call in your spirit animal for support, as we did in Chapter 1. This will not only boost your confidence to face certain situations, but it will also allow you to draw from the strength of that particular spirit animal. Whenever you need to, just visualize your spirit animal by your side, sleeping, walking, or sitting beside you and having your back.

4. CREATING AN ENERGETIC WEB

A common shamanic practice to create protection for ceremonies, as well as homes, spaces, and even whole villages, is to weave an energetic web. The traditional way to do that is to face each cardinal direction, invoking the power around the area where protection and strength are needed. Each direction is honored with a gift, such as a spray, incense, song, or something from nature. Typically, we move clockwise, invoking the spirits and forces, inviting them to protect and fill the space with loving energy.

EXERCISE: BUILD AN ENERGETIC WEB

Start with the East, then South, West, and North, followed by the Sky and the Earth. Speak ritual words for each direction to call the forces in. You can, for example, say, "Spirits of the... (East, South, West, or North) I invite you to make this space a sacred place of love, strength, protection, and healing. I thank you wholeheartedly." "Father Sky, great life, protect this space so I can open to the forces of the sky with trust, allowing your light and love to flow through me. I thank you with all my heart!" "Mother Earth, strengthen my roots to you, allowing your power and love to flow through this space. Great Mother, I thank you!" Speak intuitively what feels right.

Traditionally, cardinal directions are invoked, but you can also focus on the corners or walls of your room, inviting forces you feel connected to. You can strengthen your energetic web by placing "guardians" in the four corners of your room or around your house, channeling energy for you. Let your intention guide you to what these "guardians" could represent. For example, a crystal, a tarot card, a deity figure, an image of Jesus or Mary Magdalene, or even your own artwork that embodies the energy you want to call in.

Another way to weave the energetic web is to enter a meditative state, blessing various points around, above, and below you with a prayer and your light energy. If you call the spirits in for a ceremony, make sure to release them in gratitude afterward. If you call them in for constant protection, just remember to renew the blessing from time to time.

SEVEN WAYS TO CLEAR YOUR ENERGY FIELD

The next important key to keeping an effortless energy flow is spiritual hygiene. There are many different ways in which your energetic field can get distorted, polluted, weakened, or drained, especially when you work with people. As an empath, you naturally tend to absorb other people's energies, and even if that gets significantly less with you becoming more and more empowered and trained in your gift, it's still important for your energetic well-being to recharge and cleanse properly whenever needed. So here are my most useful tips for keeping your energy field fresh and clean and your high vibrational psychic energies flowing.

1. DEEP BREATHING

Deep breathing is one of the most fundamental and impactful methods to purify your body. You might've heard that most of us use only a fraction of our actual lung capacity for most of our waking time, even though there are many benefits to conscious deep breathing. In addition to its physical benefits, breathing offers profound spiritual advantages that can enhance our overall well-being and hold the opportunity to connect with the greater oversoul. This way, we can tap into deep wisdom, thus replenishing our energy field with the highest frequencies.

This spiritual aspect of deep breathing brings a sense of inner peace, harmony, and alignment with the divine. It allows us to release stagnant energy, invite positivity, and cultivate a deeper connection to ourselves and the world around us. To increase the effects of deep breathing, sighing while exhaling helps to let go even deeper and cleanse the energy field from within. Setting multiple alarms throughout the day can serve as an easy reminder to prioritize and practice deep breathing so that we can gradually train ourselves to deepen our average breathing with time.

2. TAKING A SHOWER

Whenever you feel that your energy flow is blocked and suspect energetical clutter in your auric field, you can do an effective quick cleanse by simply taking a shower. Water is the element of cleansing, purification, and healing. It has been honored as such by many wisdom traditions. Letting it run freely over our being flushes away any energetical dirt and helps tune into the flow of life, the eternal exchange of energy.

Take a shower whenever you feel uninspired and disconnected from the divine or your higher self. Cleanse your energy field and listen. If you can do a cleansing ritual in a river, that's even more powerful! Here, the water will present itself with all its aliveness, carrying the force of nature, ready to nurture and heal. If taking a shower or bathing is inconvenient or impossible in a specific situation where you need a cleanse, you can also perform this ritual in your mind, calling on the power of the element water to purify your energy body.

3. SHAKING

While any movement can help you clean your field, shaking is an extremely effective way to immediately release energy from the system and body whenever you feel the need. Shaking can be highly effective when facing a stuck emotion and can generally help to release any unwanted energy. To increase its effect, you can start by centering and grounding yourself. Then, deepen your breathing and connect to the sensations of being inside your body.

Now, begin gently micro-shaking the specific body parts that require it or even your entire body. Feel into yourself, and determine which shaking intensity feels right for you at the moment. Micro shaking can feel especially relaxing, while other times, you might need to get up and shake stronger. Get your cells to vibrate and feel how the unwanted energy is shaken out of your nervous system, relieving all tension. This technique is my personal favorite when it comes to releasing energy from the system and body. Since I started doing it regularly, my life energy flows much more freely and powerfully, so I recommend doing it as frequently as you feel inspired.

Note: If you'd like to go wild and want supportive music, find a playlist for this exercise in our Spotify bundle.

4. SMUDGING

Herbal smudges are a traditional way of clearing spiritual energy in people and their auric fields. Shamans know many different ways to smudge, for example, with or without accompanying chanting, with different movements and various herbs, such as white sage, palo santo, or rosemary.

To begin, you can experiment with smudging along your auric field or even individually smudge each chakra. You can also do an invocation or use toning and singing to amplify your intention. Feel free to be creative and intuitively explore which method feels right for you at the moment. Besides that, smudging is a way of cleansing the air and a great technique to infuse the space with specific qualities if you choose to. You can focus solely on the cleansing aspect or invite energies like strength, happiness, joy, or pleasure.

5. SENDING AWAY WHAT'S NOT YOURS

As an empath, you have no problem listening to someone else's problem until it's stuck with you and draining your energy—sometimes even after you return home. In those cases and generally, to cleanse off the outside world when you return to your safe home space, you can send energy back to its origin.

EXERCISE: SENDING AWAY ENERGY THAT'S NOT YOURS

Find a moment of calm where you can close your eyes and be undistracted. Connect to your self-love and let your healthy anger arise from there, acknowledging that you are worthy of peace. Then focus on your energy field and state in your mind or, to make it even more powerful, out loud: "I am sending away all energies that don't belong to me with love and respect for all. With authority, I fill my space with my own energy, and may all energy that doesn't belong to me return to its origin." Then, use your hands to wash your aura, envisioning a white light from your palm that cleanses all energetic dirt from your field.

6. CALLING BACK YOUR POWER

Just as powerful as sending energy back is regularly recalling your own energy from all external attachments back into your field. This will recenter your energy within yourself and fill your cup back up whenever you feel depleted. Practicing this exercise regularly can help you strengthen your energetic boundaries, protect your energy from external influences, and promote a greater sense of self-awareness and well-being.

EXERCISE: CALLING BACK YOUR POWER

Find a quiet and comfortable space to relax and close your eyes to prevent any distractions. Take a few deep breaths to center yourself and enter a state of calmness. Once you feel relaxed, bring your attention to your energy field. Imagine it as a radiant sphere of light surrounding your body, extending a few inches beyond your physical form. Visualize this energy field as vibrant and strong. As you focus on your energy field, repeat the following affirmation either aloud or silently in your mind: "I call my power back to me.

I reclaim all aspects of my energy and bring them back into myself."

As you recite the affirmation, feel a deep connection with your energy field. Imagine it as a magnetic force that begins to draw back any scattered or dispersed energy from external sources. Envision all energetic attachments returning to you and all energetic leaks closing so your energy field is completely replenished. With each breath, imagine the energy returning to you, revitalizing and recharging your entire being. Allow yourself to feel a sense of empowerment and inner strength as your energy field becomes more centered and whole.

7. CUTTING ENERGETIC CORDS WHEN NECESSARY

Another way to clean your field is to cut energy cords to people that might be draining you. As we discussed in the previous chapter, this will point toward an underlying shadow issue within yourself that caused you to bond with the person in an unhealthy or unwanted way. Your souls are still connected because there are unresolved feelings or lessons to be learned between you. Such a bond exists as an energetic cord in the subtle realms.

You know you are truly ready to cut the cord when you feel forgiveness towards yourself, that person, and your shared past. But you can also use this exercise to cut the connection bit by bit. Detaching from the other person might not be a one-time thing but a journey that can take time. Give it all the time it needs. If you wish to, you can ask for forgiveness in return. Then, cut the cord with love, knowing that you can still be connected through true soul love if you want to.

EXERCISE: CUTTING CORDS

Visualize the energetic cord running between you and them and make the conscious decision to cut this cord. Take time to journal or meditate on the type of contract your soul might've agreed on with the other one's soul to figure out what ties you to them. Oftentimes, we need clarity before we can find peace and closure.

To figure out the details of that soul contract, ask yourself how this person still triggers or serves your personal soul growth. Are there any lessons for you to learn in this situation? What need might still be fulfilled by the presence of this person, and is there a healthier way of fulfilling this need? Is there anything that still wants to be seen or felt? Get clear on why you want to cut it, and then either in your mind or out loud, say, "I wish to cut this cord." A physical movement of cutting through the connection with your hands can support you in the process. Explain to them that you feel grateful for the soul lesson they brought into your life but that you'd like to draw back your energy and finish the lesson without being connected to them from here on.

FIVE WAYS TO CREATE A HIGH VIBRATIONAL
HOME ENVIRONMENT

Another important aspect of spiritual hygiene in energy work is creating the right environment. As an empath, you are extremely sensitive to your surroundings. One big part of caring for your energy is creating a supportive, nurturing, and safe environment where your abilities can flow and blossom. Empaths are likely to be more sensitive to the aesthetics that surround them. This is a gift since it means that you can sense what energies the objects around you carry. Clutter, for example, might feel constraining to you and drain your energy field. On the other hand, you've probably experienced an uplift in energy when surrounded by beautiful scenery.

Empaths often unconsciously pick up on the energy of their surroundings. You can use this to your advantage to build an environment with the highest possible frequency. For this, you can use the following five steps:

1. CLEANING OUT THE SPACE

Cleaning is an important way to maintain the energy of your space. You might have experienced it before, but once you finally clean up that desk and sit down to relax, the creative drought ends, and a sudden flash of inspiration hits you. Other times, you might have gotten stuck in feeling blue for a few days. And noticing how the space around you became messier the more your motivation dropped. Cleaning up after having felt depressed for a while always feels like a reset, a fresh start. Because energetically, it is. When energy builds up in a space, it blocks the natural flow of things and hinders new energies from entering. That means fewer ideas, less creative inspiration, and fewer blessings from the universe.

Inviting the divine into your space is a matter of showing appreciation and making it comfortable for the higher energies. So, make it a habit to clean your spiritual ritual and meditation space and declutter regularly. Try to become more minimalistic with your possessions and make it a point to fill your space only with things that match your energy and desired frequency. Feel into every object and question whether this needs to be with you or whether it might just fill out your field and maybe even block the way for new things that want to come to you. Ask yourself: Does this item give me positive energy? If not, let it go and free up the space.

2. FILLING IT WITH THE RIGHT VIBES

Make sure the furniture and objects you choose to enhance your space are aesthetically pleasing to you. It's not always just about practicality; the divine likes beauty as well, and the more enjoyable your place is, the more high vibrational energy will want to be around. Make sure you use figures and symbols embodying the exact right energy for you. If it resonates with you, use candles to invite the element of fire into your space, infused room spray to invite the element of water, crystals to invite the element of earth, or smudge to invite the element of air. Use incense to infuse the air with your favorite quality, for example, a scent that lightens your mood and fills your room with warmth, lightness, and freshness.

If you work with certain spirits, you might use their favorite scent to invite their presence into the room. You can also play high-frequency music, such as binaural beats or shamanic drums, which can uplift a room's energy. See how the energy around you takes on different forms to play with you and how you can influence the atmosphere. All these things are ways of honoring the fact that we interact with the divine by connecting to the surrounding field. Whatever will make you feel most comfortable and happy will also be the most inviting to the divine and your highest possible frequency.

3. CONSCIOUS CLOTHING

As an empath, you are also likely more sensitive to the clothes you wear. Wearing the right colors that raise your vibration can greatly increase your attitude to life. The same goes for clothing made of a comfortable fabric that does not constrict your body anywhere. A super soft cotton top can work wonders compared to a cheap one. The soft fabric caresses the skin and can seem like a declaration of love to your body.

Knowledge of the energy of shapes, colors, and materials is ancient. There's a reason why most shamans had and still have certain ceremonial clothing and face paint for their rituals. Certain colors and shapes invite certain energies. For example, if you have plans to go out, you might get an immediate and excited boost of energy after putting on your red dress while getting a more peaceful and grounding energy by putting on your brown dress.

If you have the chance, investing in proper comfy clothes that make your body feel at ease and lift your overall frequency can be a worthwhile act of self-love. So next time you shop for clothes, ask yourself what will make your body and soul feel good. Your clothing should fit all your individual needs.

4. CONSCIOUS CONSUMPTION

Another way to fill your space with good vibrations is conscious consumption. What you consume influences the space and, of course, the vibration in your own energy field, which in turn influences the space. We often underestimate how much the things we consume and invite into our space influence our energy field and our direct surroundings.

This is true for any information or energy we take into our being, be it on a physical, emotional, mental, or spiritual level. Therefore, it is highly beneficial to become aware of what you consume regularly, perhaps even daily. Are you consuming things that are enhancing and lifting your energy? Or are you consuming things that are heavy on your system? If you watch the news regularly, try to observe how it makes you feel and figure out which information you need to take in. What kind of entertainment are you engaging in? Stuff that helps you grow and relaxes your system? Or stuff that kills your time and motivation? Are you feeding yourself junk? Or are you eating and drinking foods that nourish your cells and promote health? Also, what kind of people do you surround yourself with? Do they gossip a lot or uplift you and open your heart?

In the beginning, it might not feel good to acknowledge what we feed ourselves; it might hurt to take an honest look at it. But the more conscious you become of what energy you consume and how it makes you feel, the more intuitively you will adjust these habits to things that make you feel better and enhance your quality of life. This can take time, of course; always be gentle with yourself! If it's hard for you to let go of old habits, bring your focus to the new habits you want to invite into your life. With time, they will replace the old ones, and this will raise your energy level enormously.

5. BEING AWARE OF THE RESIDENTIAL SURROUNDINGS

Ideally, you choose your residential surroundings consciously as well, meaning you watch out for what houses, people, and general energy surround you, whether there is a lot of traffic, noise, a lot of businesses with stressed workers, or maybe rather some peaceful nature and forest in your immediate surrounding. The overall energy pool in which you reside greatly influences the energies that enter your field. If there is a lot of stressful energy around you, you will perceive that whenever you are open. This is why so many people reach lasting healing only when they leave the environment that makes them sick.

If you find yourself constantly exhausted, drained, and struggling to recharge properly, even when you withdraw into your space, it might be worth considering a change of environment or start working toward that. In the long run, you will notice a huge difference in life quality when you move into an area with a high frequency, such as a place close to nature or a community of like-minded individuals. Suppose you don't have the option to relocate, or while you are waiting to move, it also helps to find a peaceful, nurturing place somewhere around, like a bench in a park, a tree in the forest that you can lean against, or another place that you feel strengthens your energy field.

THE BORN HEALER

*T*his chapter is dedicated to understanding the healing process and what it means to be a healer. To me, a healer is anyone who provides an impulse to restore a state of health and balance in any situation. Since we all originate from a place of balance and wholeness on a soul level, the path to healing is always a return—taking away what has been distracting from the underlying truth of eternal harmony.

Anyone who supports this process becomes an assistant for this universal journey back to wholeness. And since it is a natural law that everything always returns to a state of balance when it's unhindered, as a healer, you don't even need to do much more than to understand what is blocking healing from happening and then help release that blockage. The best you can do to help anyone is to open a sacred healing space for them to help themselves. This is what it truly means to hold space for others—allowing their own innate processes to unfold and supporting them through their journey.

To do that, you don't need to work in a healing profession. There are many different forms of healers on this Earth, some of them working as energy readers, psychics, medicine people, counselors, and spiritual guides, but also Earth keepers like gardeners, who take care of their own piece of land or even entertainers who help brighten up people's mood.

In truth, anyone becomes a healer by sending the right impulse to the right person and, thereby triggering a change in perspective and inspiring the self-healing journey. That can be by something as simple as listening to a stranger at the bus stop or finding the right words for a friend who is in a difficult situation. The most impactful healing can get triggered by the small moments in life.

Anyone can step into the calling to be a healer in their own unique way and facilitate love and harmony—the highest divine frequencies. And the most important person to heal is always yourself. By becoming your own healed version, you'll automatically send vibrations of love and wholeness into your world, inspiring others around you to do the same. You'll become a beacon of light, illuminating even the darkest places. So whether you work in a healing profession or not, the tips in this chapter can greatly benefit how you navigate life as an empath since being a healer is the ultimate coming together of your empathic powers and gifts.

THE ANATOMY OF HEALING

Before we look deeper into what makes an empowered healer, let's first understand the healing mechanism. What happens when we heal, and how do we get there?

Whenever we talk about healing in the most general sense, we usually mean the return to a state where our well-being is uncompromised, and we rest in a deep sense of peace. In most cases, that means freedom from heavy emotions that are stored in our field and disrupt or block our natural flow of energy and unconditional love. If not released, these blockages eventually manifest as physical ailments or mental health conditions.

As we have discussed in the previous chapters, our thoughts, habits, and beliefs create our world—and therefore also our illnesses—often from the unconscious. Healing means recognizing the harmful patterns that are stored there and gaining an understanding of the underlying wounds.

The process that has proven to be most effective for me and my clients, especially Empaths, is being compassionately present with and feeling through the stored emotion in our body and following our intuitive intelligence to discover what is needed in a certain moment. That could, for example, look like traveling back in time to the helpless, wounded version of ourselves and offering what was needed. Maybe there's an emotion that's stuck and needs to be expressed, maybe our voice needs to be freed, or maybe our body needs to move to release tension. Our system already knows how to heal, and we need patience and trust to follow that intuitive guidance. It's important to note that the process of healing, as well as the approach to healing, can look very different for different people, and there is no right way to heal. Through healing, our harmful patterns loosen their grip on us and, over time, get replaced by healthy ones.

So, especially in trauma work, the first step in healing is to figure out the root trauma that is creating patterns in our lives and see how it influences the particular illness or symptom we want to treat. We can use different tools, such as general observation and asking questions, to get this understanding. But since the trauma is often stored in our subconscious, you will soon find that interrogating the conscious might not get you to the root of the issue.

This is where your empathic and psychic skills are beneficial because they allow you to read the underlying energy patterns directly by sensing where you or the system across from you is reactive. Depending on which clairsense you're using, you might feel, hear, or see it. While the conscious mind often tells a whole story, we can suddenly perceive deep vibrations or sentiments with a specific sentence or statement. This is the way to go. Repeat these sentences, ask questions about them, and try to describe what you have noticed. Expand the feeling by breathing into it.

After identifying the energetic patterns we want to change, the next step is to acknowledge them. If you find that the root issue is a subconscious belief of "I am not enough," you want to spend time with that part of yourself that feels that way, feel with it, and give it love and acceptance. Thereby, you open up to a deeper level of healing.

Whenever a wounded part of you connects to love, another part of the soul returns and brings wholeness. Here, inner child and soul meditations can be very useful tools. Working with specific affirmations that feel empowering and healing will help you install new vibrations in your energy field.

Since healing happens in spirals, you'll find that the more you heal, the deeper the layers you discover, and that is exactly how the process is supposed to unfold; it's the nature of life itself. An ongoing process of discovering yourself and embodying more and more of your wholeness as you move along.

Healing does not mean that the wounds simply disappear; healing means being aware of the wound, noticing it, breathing with it, and facing it with a capacity that can hold and regulate it. The pain will then no longer have a negative impact on our life and well-being. It might still be there, but it gets balanced by our growing capacity to hold ourselves.

The more you progress on your healing path, the more you will learn to be centered in the part of you that could never be hurt: your soul. This place within us that is and has always been whole, powerful, and full of divine love.

The part of us that embraces and holds our injured human part with compassion, warmth, love, and confidence at all times. It is in the arms of our soul that the human heart finds healing. With this support and the love and awareness that flows through you, your wounds lose their negative effect on your life.

Then we experientially remember the eternal truth behind this physical world: that we've been whole all along. We can open to the divine source frequency, which soothes the human wounds with its sweet nectar of unconditional love and repairs all damage so that our being returns to its optimal state.

Over time, you will discard old destructive behaviors and adopt new healthy ones. You'll increasingly start to care for yourself and move toward a happier life, relieved of heavy baggage.

Healing is a process that occurs naturally when we infuse our reality with harmonious instead of disruptive frequency patterns. That can be a new self-care routine, retreating to reconnect to ourselves and our soul, rest, or finding a particular therapy that fits us. The more harmonious and wholesome your thoughts, words, and deeds, the more harmonious and wholesome your emotional state, body, and environment will become.

And then there is another even deeper aspect of healing. Understanding and claiming the gift, the skill that grew from mastering this painful life experience. Because, as shaman traditions point out, anything that happens in life comes to tell or teach us something. Healing is not only finding the path back to one's own soul but, on the way, also collecting what you have learned and bringing it home. And the ultimate skill you will gain from healing yourself is the awakening of your own inner infinitely wise healer.

THE WOUNDED HEALER

Everybody can be a healer, and the best healers are those who've experienced their subjects' pain firsthand.

You might've heard about the legend of the wounded healer before. Chiron was a centaur. Half human, half horse. But he was also a god—so when he got hit by a poisoned arrow, he didn't just die like a human most probably would have but was left with an incurable eternal wound that wouldn't heal. Unable to live with the constant pain, he saw himself forced to invent a cure, and so he did. And suddenly, he knew how to cure everyone.

As we often find with myths, they not only inspire our imagination but also point us toward a dormant potential within ourselves. In this case, it's the inherent human potential to become a healer by suffering a seemingly incurable disease. In this way, many healers are born by becoming experts in their own conditions and examining them in the closest way possible—firsthand. Another crucial aspect of this story is the compassion Chiron felt for those who suffered the same pain he did. Seeing others go through what we have gone through motivates us to share what we have discovered during our own healing.

The story of Chiron teaches us that by solving our own issues, we can tap into a sacred calling—to channel this healing into the world and support others in doing the same. And that from a soul perspective, a devastating diagnosis, trauma, injury, or loss can be a powerful invitation to awaken our inherent healing abilities. From a shamanic perspective, these are powerful initiations arranged by our soul and our spirit guides who want to activate us into fulfilling our calling and realizing our full potential. Some shamanic traditions even say that a destined healer who ignores their calling will suffer tremendously until they surrender to their higher destiny, cure themselves, and become the healer they were meant to be.

As the legendary myth of the wounded healer teaches us, our greatest purpose can often be found in the crossline between our deepest pain and our greatest gift. So, the wound you carry within yourself is a strong indicator of the gift that you have to share with others. Once you give in to the calling, you will find that by healing yourself, you will automatically be much more capable of supporting others in their healing and naturally step into your healer role.

As the path of healing is a never-ending, continuous process, you will reach a higher level of resilience, understanding, and wisdom with each step of your journey. And with each step, you will gain a new tool that can also be a possible solution for others who experience similar life challenges. So please, never think you have to wait to be able to share your gifts with others! The mere fact that you are reading this book already shows that you have taken significant steps on your way, even if it doesn't feel like it yet. You have something to offer to this world!

Through giving, we enter the next level of our own journey and experience an even deeper layer of healing. Because now, we recognize how much it is that we have to give and how powerful we are in influencing our surroundings. We rediscover our creative energy, and through creating healing spaces for others, we heal ourselves, too.

When we open healing spaces, for ourselves or for others, huge power and love flows through us that often feels much bigger than we as humans could ever contain. This energy is the One, the beginning, and the end. And all of us can turn into channels for that power. It is a grace—for ourselves and others—when this power is allowed to flow freely through us. It is one of the greatest gifts, and we can give thanks with reverence.

Your unique medicine is most likely a mixture of the cure of your pain and your passions. On my own journey, for example, I struggled with the deep pain of never feeling good enough for many years. The remedy for this anguish was unconditional love and appreciation towards myself. I embarked on a journey to invoke these emotions, delving into inner child work. Because writing, filmmaking, and inspiring others have always been passions of mine, I began sharing my discoveries on Instagram and YouTube, which eventually evolved into a profession as I started offering individual sessions and seminars to help people through the same challenges I had gone through.

After a few years, I realized a new wound needed attention – the pain in my inner child that no one had ever believed in my grand dreams. I navigated ways to heal and renewed my faith in even the most audacious aspirations. In doing so, I rediscovered my passion and gift for leadership and founded WhereDreamsManifest, a company dedicated to turning dreams into reality. This shows that our special abilities can evolve as time passes. At various points in our lives, different strengths and talents within us seek expression. Another interesting aspect emerges here: our greatest gifts are often a mixture of the qualities that have been most recognized and praised in our childhood and the qualities that have been most devalued or ridiculed.

But of course, every path is unique, and it is important to note that someone's unique medicine does not always have to become a career as it did for me. One of my clients searched for a long time for her calling because she thought it would have to become her career. In our session, we found that her greatest pain lay in living in a world that was often so hard and had so rarely shown her compassion and gentleness. But her greatest pain was also her greatest gift, as she never stopped feeling deeply with everyone.

She realized that she was already happy with her traditional desk job and just wanted to focus more on bringing her medicine into her workspace as well as just acknowledging how much she had already given. She found her greatest calling in sharing her love with the world and herself in all the little everyday moments. Her unique medicine became a way of living life completely independent of her profession and career. Another client was working as a kindergarten teacher and was able to channel her own inner child healing into her work with children, igniting a deep fulfillment and passion for her job.

However you decide to integrate your unique medicine into your life is totally up to you, and it will look different for everyone. But whatever it is that heals you will likely also transform other areas of your life, as it leads to a kind of deeper meaning and peace that makes you feel like you have unlocked a deeper level of your own destiny.

The questions in the following exercise can give you valuable insights into what that personal medicine could be in your case. As discovered, your answers might not be final; they can change with time. So, it could be beneficial to answer these questions every couple of years.

EXERCISE: FIND YOUR UNIQUE MEDICINE

Find a quiet spot where you won't be disturbed, and have a piece of paper and a pen ready to write down the answers that come to you.

When you're ready, connect to your breathing. Breathe out noisily a few times and let go of all your everyday thoughts. When you feel deeply relaxed, imagine the radiant light of your soul essence and bathe in your own divine presence for a few moments. Let yourself sink into the deep stillness, the deep peace of your soul, and connect with the deep wisdom that dwells within.

Then, start asking the following questions into this wide space and listen to what answers arise. Take time for each question—the answer may be more complex or even more simple than you think.

What is my deepest pain?

What is the cure for this pain?

How can I bring this cure to myself?

What are my gifts and passions?

What do I love doing?

When do I feel most in flow with life?

How can I combine my passions with the cure of my pain?

How can I let my medicine flow into this world effortlessly?

Ask your soul who you are and what you want to embody. For what did you choose this life? Perceive the image of your soul, of all the light that you brought with you into this life. Connect and anchor all messages, feelings, and pictures that you perceive from your soul into a movement or certain posture. You can adopt this posture repeatedly, getting back into contact with your essence and calling more quickly.

If you find it difficult to answer the above questions, or as a valuable addition, you can ask those close to you what they see as your unique medicine. You can also make it a habit to ask your soul at night before you go to sleep: "How does my medicine want to flow into my life? Please reveal it to me." And for the following weeks, observe what shows up in your dreams and waking life.

TRAITS OF AN EMPOWERED HEALER

Now, to give you a good summary of qualities that you can cultivate to be an empowered healer and conscious empath, here are seven traits that great healers hold. It is important to say that nobody ever fulfills all these characteristics one hundred percent. This is not even possible; after all, we are and remain human. Therefore, this enumeration should only offer a clue which aspects to consider in self-reflection to grow further into your true greatness as a healer. With that being said, let's take a look at what makes an empowered healer.

1. THEY FILL THEIR OWN CUP FIRST

Experienced healers know an empty hand has nothing to give. If you want to inspire people with wholesome, divine healing energy, you cannot pour from an empty cup. You'll need to charge up your own batteries first; every healing work starts with a proper self-care routine. Especially for empaths, this is a must and should never be compromised on. That extra mile that you like to run for others, even though you can feel your batteries running low, has to stop!

In the beginning, it might feel hard, even selfish, to put yourself first, especially when you're surrounded by people who seem to need help. But in truth, the exact opposite is the case. On the one hand, by taking care of yourself, you empower others to learn the same and to recognize that they, too, can be there for themselves. This can be a great gift for them, even if it doesn't feel like it at first. On the other hand, after some time of withdrawal, you will notice that your energy has much more to offer to others. You can now be there for them with genuine, selfless support because you are less triggered or drained by them and can, therefore, give unconditionally and with more resources.

Learn to check in with yourself first before you dedicate any energy to your surroundings. You are still your most important healing subject. A tiny adjustment on your own path, a proper refill on your own being, can make a massive difference in the quality and quantity of high vibrational energy you'll have to share with the world. Refilling yourself is a constant and continuous process that demands your awareness and your time, reflecting on your experiences and what wants to be integrated, especially after doing energy work with others.

So, instead of budgeting your finite energy, why not focus on filling yourself so much till you resemble an overflowing cup of healing energy? Then, you are in tune with your divine energy source and can offer abundantly without effort.

2. THEY ARE HONEST WITH THEMSELVES AND OTHERS

Honesty and transparency are the next important traits of an authentic healer. To see what is needed to bring healing into a certain situation, things must be clear for yourself and those you might work with. It creates the necessary trust to open up and more importantly: you need to be able to trust yourself. As a healer, you are a facilitator of truth because seeing the truth can help a disrupted situation return to peace and balance.

Learn more and more to communicate honestly, even when it feels scary. As long as you connect the spoken truth to your heart and compassion, it will always bring healing, despite how uncomfortable it feels in the moment. That means you need to face your own shadows, weaknesses, and subconscious beliefs, and you need to be honest about them with yourself and others.

A conscious healer knows that they carry their own stories, past wounds, and how they can get projected onto others. They try to be as open as possible about their weaknesses, which enables them to move past their personal stories and devote themselves to acting solely on the well-being of others. It's not always easy to be fully transparent with others or yourself. It takes courage to be seen as who you are, but the more you embody your honest self, the deeper the trust you will experience between yourself, your client, and the whole existence.

3. THEY BECOME A SACRED WITNESS

As an empath, you possess the natural ability to be present and listen with your whole being, whether that be listening to someone else's story, to your own inner child, to the divine, or to spirits that want to communicate information to you. You listen with more than just your ears; you're able to feel what is being conveyed. And that is another great strength of every empowered healer, knowing that every problem, by nature, holds its solution inherent, hidden in plain sight—ready for us to discover if we'll just listen. Most of the time, the problem is not a lack of possible solutions but rather that the person is so stuck in their energy that they can't see and attract the solution. This is why we often find that talking about our problems—even if the other person is just listening—enables us to find clarity we didn't have access to before because it lets our energy flow again.

How often have you experienced that while ranting about your situation to a friend, you realized that you know exactly what to do about it; you just haven't taken the time to puzzle everything together? You just needed someone to witness the process of dissecting the problem. And this is what a healer often does. But even if your client doesn't realize the solution on their own, asking the right questions is often the best assistance we can provide. Here, it is essential to mention that it is not about finding a solution at all in many cases, but the solution often lies in simply allowing the current process to be present. Long-term solutions will automatically emerge from that. To get a full bird's-eye view of the situation, it is necessary to step into your greatest wisdom, your inner knowing. By opening up to your higher consciousness, you become a sacred witness to your subject and infuse the situation with divine awareness. This is where all the answers can be found, and where healing starts to unfold.

Being a sacred witness means knowing what you are witnessing is sacred. It means recognizing the other person as a part of the holy creation. You hold the certainty of the greatness and light of the other person's soul, even if they may not see it themselves at the moment. At the same time, you hold the certainty of their humanity and acknowledge everything that belongs to them. You recognize and hold the other person in their entirety while allowing them to fully immerse themselves in one of these aspects with deep compassion. To feel deeply, release pent-up emotions, and consequently, inevitably recognize the other aspects of their being.

4. THEY KNOW THEY ARE NOT RESPONSIBLE FOR EVERYONE

Even though you might develop a strong desire to help everyone out of their misery as an empath and awakened healer, you will soon find that not everyone can be helped. In fact, not everyone even wants to be helped. Because not everyone is ready to start and commit to their own healing journey, and that is something you can never decide for people. They have to make that decision themselves; only then can you step in to assist them. Everyone has their own path, and everyone's soul has their perfect, divinely timed awakening. This is something to remember in your service to the world and other souls.

Also, remember that you don't have the right medicine for every person. Someone might seek healing from you and be open but still struggle to get better with your guidance. In such cases, it is crucial for an empowered healer to recognize their own limitations and acknowledge that they are not all-knowing and that their unique medicine doesn't always suits everybody's needs or personal truth.

These situations are opportunities to show true greatness by encouraging people to seek their healing through alternative paths or with other individuals. In doing so, we should remind them and us that it's no one's fault or failure but simply a matter of misalignment and that the right medicine is waiting for them somewhere. Realize that there are people in this world who need your exact medicine right now but cannot reach you if you are filling your energy field with people for whom your medicine is not right.

5. THEY ARE IN SERVICE TO OTHERS

From a place of compassion and unconditional love arises the healer's desire to serve the higher good and, therefore, others. Since they fill their own cup first, connecting themselves to universal love and centering themselves in the unified field of oneness when it comes to their work, true healers leave their own personal desires and interests aside and focus on how they can best assist the person in need—not by effort but by feeling so fulfilled and overflowing with love that they simply start to want to improve the lives of everyone around them.

Their desire to heal results from deep gratitude and the wish to share the healing they themselves have received, as well as a deep understanding of oneness, acknowledging that the people around them are always an extension of themselves on a soul level. For true healers, their work in itself is an honor and highly sacred because they know with every deed, they are acting on behalf of the highest divine energy and are, therefore, divinely guided and supported, helping others to connect to that source of healing themselves. Your intention should, therefore, always be to give what is needed instead of what your expectations tell you to give.

6. THEY KEEP THEIR HUMILITY

An awakened healer will always be humble toward the fact that we are never all-knowing and can be mistaken at any time. They keep their humility towards the great mystery of the universe, knowing that they can never grasp it entirely.

An empowered healer will, therefore, keep a sense of humbleness toward the perspectives of others, meaning that they respect others' own authority about their experiences, feelings, and needs. The best healers are those who support others to awaken their own healing capabilities as well as their own inner wisdom and encourage them to trust their own authority and intuition.

They know they merely create a healing space that allows people to connect to themselves and their own powers. That's because awakened healers acknowledge that, ultimately, deep down, we all know what is best for our own system and are the only ones who can decide what feels right and proper to us. So, the very best you can offer as a healer is your experienced knowledge and your personal perspective while at the same time retaining your humility to not knowing better than the individual themselves.

After all, there are infinite realms, dimensions, and truths–so how could we ever claim to know the absolute truth?

7. THEY TRUST IN THEIR POWER AND INTUITION

In my own experience, the number of people I could accompany on their journey grew bigger and bigger the deeper I healed myself. But even in the early beginnings of my healing path, there were people who needed the exact medicine that I could give at that time. I always automatically attracted precisely those who needed my help. So, even though the key to unlocking your power lies in healing yourself, don't fall into the trap of thinking you must be fully healed to help others! Because that's unrealistic. Maybe there will always be a part of our human self that doesn't feel healed, which, however, has nothing to do with how much we have to give.

This point was especially important for me because I see so many talented people who would have so much to give and could do it with joy and ease, yet they aren't allowing themselves to do so because they think they first have to be further on their journey. And if you are at this point, I would like to tell you: This is far from the truth! You are ready! Open yourself to it and see how it flows into your life all on its own, and watch your powers unfold.

Of course, you also don't need to pressure yourself to share your gifts. If you live and explore them just for yourself, that is already enough to heal the world around you. Just don't hesitate to share your light if you feel called to!

MY MESSAGE FOR YOU

Being an empath in our world surely isn't easy, and even though you might've gone through serious challenges in your life, I'm sure that something in you always knew that your abilities and sensitivities were special. I sincerely hope that this book could help you realize the beauty and magic of being able to perceive life so fully.

If you are one of those empaths who haven't found their soul family yet and maybe feel somewhat misplaced in this society, I just want to tell you: You are not alone! Even if it feels like that sometimes. There are many of us! Just take one step at a time on your path, and we will all find each other! And this is your world, too, and you carry the gift within you that it so des perately needs. So, let's create a new reality together filled with profound compassion! You are deeply loved. I see you. And it's time to realize who you are and to embrace your greatness! It's time to become the hero that you've always needed!

With this book, I hope I have given you both inspiration and tools to explore all your hidden treasures. Now it's time to unpack the magic that lives in you! Both in the dark and in the light. In your strengths as well as in your weaknesses. In your psychic abilities as well as in your shadows. Allow yourself to show your shadows openly and vulnerably, embracing them in love, and let your abilities radiate freely and wildly. You truly deserve it!

Always be gentle with yourself and celebrate your humanity as much as your divinity. We will probably never be fully empowered, and at the same time, we are becoming more empowered every day. And isn't that the greatest adventure? The path of learning, growing, healing, and transforming, and the chance to fall in love anew every day.

Now that you've seen all the ways in which you can access your inherent power, it's time to put these practices to the test and invite all the magic into your life. Remember to always feel into yourself and into your own truth. And with all the healing talk, don't forget that you didn't come here only to heal. You came to enjoy life, marvel, and explore all the breathtaking mysteries of existence.

Whatever path you choose for yourself, make sure to follow your intuition and trust life. Everything will happen exactly as it should and within divine timing.

There is so much more to being an empath that I couldn't fit into this book. You will keep discovering new knowledge and ways to expand your capabilities. This book could hopefully give you a glimpse of what's possible and inspire you to connect with yourself and your powers. Have fun experimenting with what else you can discover!

If you haven't already made use of my special offer, here's your last reminder to benefit from the free meditation and Spotify package to support and complement the exercises in this book. To get the download link, just go to:

www.wheredreamsmanifest.com/empath

If you liked this book, I would greatly appreciate it if you could share your experience in an Amazon review to help other souls find my work as well. I read every single review, and it always warms my heart to hear about your journeys and experiences! On the next page, you will find a QR Code that will get you there directly.

Thank you so much for your support 🙏

I wish you all the best on your journey!

So much love,

Sanyana

SHARE YOUR EMPOWERMENT

DEAR BEAUTIFUL EMPATH

IF YOU ENJOYED READING THIS BOOK,

PLEASE LEAVE A REVIEW TO HELP OTHERS

USA	UK	CANADA	AUSTRALIA

Simply by leaving a review on Amazon, you'll support us to spread our message and help other empaths find their empowerment as well.

We appreciate your help!
Much Love,
Sanyana and the WHERE DREAMS MANIFEST Team

Free Meditation and Spotify Bundle

Inner Child Healing

Grounding and Centering

Guided Affirmations for Empaths

The Spotify bundle includes playlists for:

Healing

Mantra Meditations

Meeting your Soul

Meeting your Inner Child

Shaking out Stuck Energies

The Candle Flame Meditation

Beautiful Meditation Backgroundmusic

Follow the link to our website or scan the QR Code down below
to get 3 beautifully guided meditations and 7 Spotify playlists.
These complement the exercises in this book and are great
for practical support for working through them.

To get the download links, go to our website:

wheredreamsmanifest.com/empath

Or scan this QR Code:

ABOUT THE AUTHOR

Sanyana Alaina is a spiritual teacher and medicine woman who has dedicated her life to helping people discover and embody the transformative power of love and open up to real-life magic. Her journey of overcoming depression, an eating disorder, and difficult family relationships has given her a deep understanding of the emotional blocks that hold people back from living fulfilling lives.

Through her unique blend of shamanic ceremonies, meditations, tantric rituals, breathwork, and coaching, Sanyana creates safe and nurturing spaces for people to explore, heal, and grow. She intuitively supports people in releasing emotional blocks, healing deep-seated wounds, and connecting to their highest inner wisdom and abilities. She believes that everyone has the capacity for deep healing and transformation and is committed to guiding others toward a life of self-love, peace, fulfillment, and joy.

So far, Sanyana's work has been known only in the German-speaking region, but with the publication of her book, she can now fulfill her dream of reaching people worldwide. She also shares her teachings on her YouTube channel, Sanyana Alaina, and her Instagram page: @sanyana_alaina, where she loves connecting with her readers in English. Whether through her book, online presence, or in-person sessions, Sanyana is dedicated to helping people discover the magic of love and live their best lives.

www.ingramcontent.com/pod-product-compliance
Lightning Source LLC
LaVergne TN
LVHW040058110925
820831LV00002B/31